3rd Edition

Ajit Singh

Data Modeling with

Featured With
CauchDB, MongoDB, Riak
HBase, Cassandra

PREFACE

As the Web continues to grow in size, more and more services are being created that require data persistence. The amount of data that these services need to archive is growing at an exponential rate and so is the amount of accesses that these services have to serve. Additionally, the relationships between data are also increasing. In the past, problems involving data persistence have been consistently solved by relying on relational databases. Still, the requirements of these new services and the needs for scalability have led to a depletion of relational database technologies. New approaches to deal with these problems have been developed and the NoSQL movement was formed. This movement fosters the creation of new non-relational databases, specialized for different problem domains, with the intent of using the "right tool for the job". Besides being non-relational, these databases also have other characteristics in common such as: being distributed, trading consistency for availability, providing easy ways to scale horizontally, etc.

A benchmarking framework was introduced in order to address the performance of NoSQL databases as well as their scalability and elasticity properties. A core set of benchmarks was defined and results are booked for three widely used systems: Cassandra, Riak and a simple sharded MySQL implementation which serves as a baseline.

This book provides a simple methodology for modeling data in a non-relational database, as well as a set of common design patterns. This book mainly focused on both Cassandra and Riak so that to fill the knowledge gap by studying the available non-relational databases in order to develop a systematic approach for solving problems of data persistence using these technologies.

Both Cassandra and Riak were able to yield good results when compared to the relational implementation used as a baseline. They also proved to be easily scalable and elastic. Cassandra, specifically, achieved significantly better results for write operations than the other systems. The developed design patterns proved themselves useful when implementing the prototypes and it is expected that given this work it will be easier to adopt a NoSQL database.

The rest of this book is structured as follows.

Chapters 2 and 3 describe the state of the art regarding, respectively, the theoretical background and technologies in the field of non-relational databases.

Chapter 4 presents the performed benchmark measurements, providing a clear interpretation of the results obtained as well as the methodology used. It also details the developed benchmarking framework.

Chapter 5 describes the acquired knowledge regarding data modeling with NoSQL databases, by exposing a simple methodology to tackle problems as well as common design patterns.

Chapter 6 introduces the domain problem that the developed prototypes will try to address in the context of the company "PT Inovação". Furthermore, it explores the two developed prototypes as well as presenting a detailed performance analysis.

Chapter 7 finishes this document by providing some conclusions about the research carried out as well as opportunities for further work.

Data Modeling with NoSQL Database

3nd Edition

Ajit Singh

CONTENTS

Chapter 1
NoSQL Introduction

With the continuous growth of the Web and an increasing reliance on the services it provides, the amount of data to archive and preserve is growing at an exponential rate. Along with the increas-ing size of the datasets, as the adoption of these services increases so does the number of accesses and operations performed. This growth, enhanced by the proliferation of social networks, led to a depletion of traditional relational databases that were commonly used to solve a wide range of problems [Lea10]. We have been witnessing a sharp growth of a set of solutions that despite differing from traditional techniques of data persistence, allow systems to cooperate with the ex-panded volume and flow of data efficiently. These solutions are based mainly in the expansion of the existing infrastructures with non-relational database systems, with the main motto being scalability.

The NoSQL movement began in early 2009 and has been growing rapidly. This movement represents a new generation of non-relational databases that share some characteristics such as: focus on the distribution of the system, scalability (mainly horizontal), non-relational schema-free representation of data, etc. Most of these new databases offer a more limited range of properties than the current RDBMS systems, relaxing consistency constraints and often not supporting full ACID properties. This relative reduction of capabilities gives the system a boost in performance, while at the same time facilitating its distribution. Still, it should be interpreted as a trade-off, which is often justified.

The name NoSQL suggests that these databases do not support the SQL query language. How-ever, it does not address their main characteristic which is the fact that they are non-relational.

The name should be interpreted as "not only sql", which suggests a change in mentality of the cur-rently employed strategies that one type of database is useful to solve all sorts of problems.

> *"The last 25 years of commercial DBMS development can be summed up in a single phrase: "One size fits all".*

Thus, this movement fosters the creation of different types of databases, each with a specific set of characteristics and applicable to different problem domains. The potential and utility of these new technologies that are under constant development and growth is unquestionable. However, after so many years modeling data using a relational approach, implementing business rules around these concepts and optimizing the outcome, a radical change of paradigm doesn't allow us to leverage the existing mass of knowledge. The potential adoption of a non-relational system is severely hampered by a lack of knowledge and expertise. The lack of knowledge and potential benefits acquired by using a NoSQL database are there-fore the main motivation for this work.

NoSQL databases are defined as non-tabular databases that handle data storage differently as compared to relational tables. NoSQL database types are classified according to the data model, and the popular types include document, graph, column, and key-value.

A NoSQL database (also known as "no SQL" or "not only SQL") is a distributed, non-relational database designed for large-scale data storage and massively parallel, high-performance data processing across many commodity systems. Unlike the traditional relational database approach, NoSQL gives you a way to work with data closer to the application. It is a modern data storage paradigm that provides data persistence for environments where high performance is the primary requirement. Within a NoSQL database, data is stored so that both writing and reading are fast, even under heavy load.

NoSQL databases are typically distributed systems where several machines work together in clusters. Each piece of data is replicated over those machines to deliver redundancy and high availability. The ability to store vast amounts of data in a distributed manner makes NoSQL databases faster to develop and deploy. NoSQL databases are built for specific data models and have flexible schemas, allowing programmers to create and manage modern applications.

A NoSQL originally referring to non SQL or non relational is a database that provides a mechanism for storage and retrieval of data. This data is modeled in means other than the tabular relations used in relational databases. Such databases came into existence in the late 1960s, but did not obtain the NoSQL moniker until a surge of popularity in the early twenty-first century. NoSQL databases are used in real-time web applications and big data and their use are increasing over time. NoSQL systems are also sometimes called Not only SQL to emphasize the fact that they may support SQL-like query languages.

A NoSQL database includes simplicity of design, simpler horizontal scaling to clusters of machines and finer control over availability. The data structures used by NoSQL databases are different from those used by default in relational databases which makes some operations faster in NoSQL. The suitability of a given NoSQL database depends on the problem it should solve. Data structures used by NoSQL databases are sometimes also viewed as more flexible than relational database tables. Many NoSQL stores compromise consistency in favor of availability, speed and partition tolerance. Barriers to the greater adoption of NoSQL stores include the use of low-level query languages, lack of standardized interfaces, and huge previous investments in existing relational databases. Most NoSQL stores lack true ACID (Atomicity, Consistency, Isolation, Durability) transactions but a few databases, such as MarkLogic, Aerospike, FairCom c-treeACE, Google Spanner (though technically a NewSQL database), Symas LMDB, and OrientDB have made them central to their designs.

Most NoSQL databases offer a concept of eventual consistency in which database changes are propagated to all nodes so queries for data might not return updated data immediately or might result in reading data that is not accurate which is a problem known as stale reads. Also some NoSQL systems may exhibit lost writes and other forms of data loss. Some NoSQL systems provide concepts such as write-ahead logging to avoid data loss. For distributed transaction processing across multiple databases, data consistency is an even bigger challenge. This is difficult for both NoSQL and relational databases. Even current relational databases do not allow referential integrity constraints to span databases. There are few systems that maintain both X/Open XA standards and ACID transactions for distributed transaction processing.

A brief history of NoSQL databases

With the start of Web 2.0, the creation of various data types exploded, and the price of storage significantly dropped, causing the challenges associated with maintaining and accessing data to shift. Relational databases, consisting of rows and columns, were designed for structured data requiring complex analysis and operations of often connected data.

With the rapid growth of unstructured data, relational databases' structural and scaling limitations came into focus. Flexibility and the ability to handle large amounts of data quickly became requirements. In the late 2000s, NoSQL databases emerged, with the advantages of storing data more intuitively and in formats that suit today's applications. NoSQL databases solve problems that can't be solved with SQL or relational databases.

- 1998- Carlo Strozzi use the term NoSQL for his lightweight, open-source relational database
- 2000- Graph database Neo4j is launched
- 2004- Google BigTable is launched
- 2005- CouchDB is launched
- 2007- The research paper on Amazon Dynamo is released
- 2008- Facebooks open sources the Cassandra project
- 2009- The term NoSQL was reintroduced

How does NoSQL work?

How does NoSQL compare? Let's take a closer look. The following NoSQL tutorial illustrates an application used for managing resumes. It interacts with resumes as an object (i.e., the user object), contains an array for skills, and has a collection for positions. Alternatively, writing a resume to a relational database requires the application to "shred" the user object.

Storing this resume would require the application to insert six rows into three tables, as illustrated in Figure 1.1.

And, reading this profile would require the application to read six rows from three tables, as illustrated in Figure 1.2.

Figure 1.1

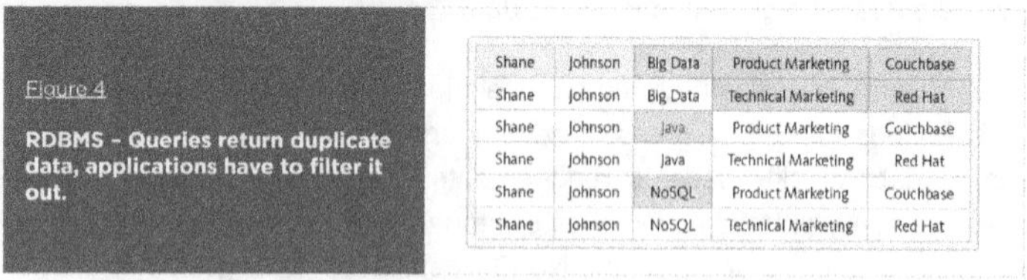

Figure-1.2

By contrast, in a document-oriented database defined as NoSQL, JSON is the de facto format for storing data – helpfully, it's also the de facto standard for consuming and producing data for web, mobile, and IoT applications. JSON not only eliminates the object-relational impedance mismatch, it also eliminates the overhead of ORM frameworks and simplifies application development because objects are read and written without "shredding" them (i.e., a single object can be read or written as a single document), as illustrated in Figure 1.3.

Figure-1.3

Businesses Use NoSQL to:

- Deploy new, innovative applications, in addition to migrating infrastructure from on-premise to cloud.
- Create data models, evaluate alternatives, find problems early, and to think through data processes.
- Satisfy the need for a very agile delivery system that is easily able to process unstructured and dynamic data.
- To prepare unstructured or "messy" data for analysis.
- Implement a scale-out architecture for high performance Data Management needs.

Features of NoSQL

1. Non-relational

- NoSQL databases never follow the relational model
- Never provide tables with flat fixed-column records
- Work with self-contained aggregates or BLOBs
- Doesn't require object-relational mapping and data normalization
- No complex features like query languages, query planners,referential integrity joins, ACID

2. Schema-free

- NoSQL databases are either schema-free or have relaxed schemas
- Do not require any sort of definition of the schema of the data
- Offers heterogeneous structures of data in the same domain

3. Simple API

- Offers easy to use interfaces for storage and querying data provided
- APIs allow low-level data manipulation & selection methods
- Text-based protocols mostly used with HTTP REST with JSON
- Mostly used no standard based NoSQL query language
- Web-enabled databases running as internet-facing services

4. Distributed

- Multiple NoSQL databases can be executed in a distributed fashion
- Offers auto-scaling and fail-over capabilities
- Often ACID concept can be sacrificed for scalability and throughput
- Mostly no synchronous replication between distributed nodes Asynchronous Multi-Master Replication, peer-to-peer, HDFS Replication
- Only providing eventual consistency
- Shared Nothing Architecture. This enables less coordination and higher distribution.

Advantages of NoSQL

Like every other technology, NoSQL databases also offer some benefits and suffer from some limitations too.

In an era where relational databases are mainly used for data storage and retrieval, modern web technologies posed a major challenge in the form of unstructured data, high scale data, enormous concurrency etc.

Relational databases struggled especially to represent highly unstructured data and high scalability and thus came into being the NoSQL databases.

Let us briefly discuss some advantages and disadvantages of NoSQL databases.

(i) Flexible Data Model

NoSQL databases are highly flexible as they can store and combine any type of data, both structured and unstructured, unlike relational databases that can store data in a structured way only.

(ii) Evolving Data Model

NoSQL databases allow you to dynamically update the schema to evolve with changing requirements while ensuring that it would cause no interruption or downtime to your application.

(iii) Elastic Scalability

NoSQL databases can scale to accommodate any type of data growth while maintaining low cost. NoSQL database use sharding for horizontal scaling. Partitioning of data and placing it on multiple machines in such a way that the order of the data is preserved is sharding. Vertical scaling means adding more resources to the existing machine whereas horizontal scaling means adding more machines to handle the data. Vertical scaling is not that easy to implement but horizontal scaling is easy to implement. Examples of horizontal scaling databases are MongoDB, Cassandra etc. NoSQL can handle huge amount of data because of scalability, as the data grows NoSQL scale itself to handle that data in efficient manner.

(iv) High Performance

NoSQL databases are built for great performance, measured in terms of both throughput (it is a measure of overall performance) and latency (it is the delay between request and actual response).

(v) Open-source

NoSQL databases don't require expensive licensing fees and can run on inexpensive hardware, rendering their deployment cost-effective.

Disadvantages of NoSQL:

NoSQL has the following disadvantages.

1. Narrow focus

NoSQL databases have very narrow focus as it is mainly designed for storage but it provides very little functionality. Relational databases are a better choice in the field of Transaction Management than NoSQL.

2. Open-source

NoSQL is open-source database. There is no reliable standard for NoSQL yet. In other words two database systems are likely to be unequal.

3. Management challenge

The purpose of big data tools is to make management of a large amount of data as simple as possible. But it is not so easy. Data management in NoSQL is much more complex than a relational database. NoSQL, in particular, has a reputation for being challenging to install and even more hectic to manage on a daily basis.

4. GUI is not available

GUI mode tools to access the database is not flexibly available in the market.

5. Backup

Backup is a great weak point for some NoSQL databases like MongoDB. MongoDB has no approach for the backup of data in a consistent manner.

6. Large document size

Some database systems like MongoDB and CouchDB store data in JSON format. Which means that documents are quite large (BigData, network bandwidth, speed), and having descriptive key names actually hurts, since they increase the document size.

Types of NoSQL database:

Types of NoSQL databases and the name of the databases system that falls in that category are;

1. **Key-value stores** are the least complex of the NoSQL databases. They are a collection of key-value pairs, and their simplicity makes them the most scalable of NoSQL databases types. Key-value can be a string, a number, and an entirely new set of key-value pairs encapsulated in an object. Use cases include shopping carts, user preferences, and leaderboards.

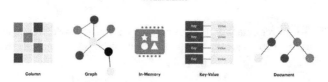

Figure-1.4 NoSQL Databases

2. **Document stores** are one step up in complexity from key-value stores. NoSQL document-based databases store information in documents with specific keys, similar to a key-value store, but with different benefits and disadvantages. Document stores appear the most natural among the NoSQL database types because they store everyday documents. They allow for complex querying and calculations on this often already aggregated form of data. Document databases store data in CML, YAML, JSON, or binary documents such as BSON. Using specific keys makes document stores similar to key-value stores. Use cases include online retail, trading platforms, and mobile app development across industries.

3. **In-memory databases** are data stores that are purpose-built to rely on DRAM for data storage to enable sub-millisecond responses. This is in contrast to most NoSQL and SQL databases that store data on disk or SSD/flash memory. It means that each time you query an in-memory database or update data in a database, you only access the main memory. There's no disk involved in these operations. And this is good, because the main memory is much faster than any disk. In-memory databases can also retain persistent data by keeping each operation on a disk in a transaction log or a snapshot. Use cases include leaderboards, session stores, and real-time analytics.

4. **Column-oriented databases** store data in tables that contain large numbers of columns (in a flexible schema). In a column-oriented database, it's easy to add another column because none of the existing columns are affected by it. Storing each column separately allows for quicker scans when only a few columns are involved. Use cases include performing analytics and reporting, including summing values and counting entries.

5. **A graph database** is the most complex data store, geared toward efficiently storing relations between entities. Graph databases are the answer when the data is highly interconnected, such as social networks, scientific paper citations, or capital asset clusters. Use cases include fraud detection, social networks, and knowledge graphs.

What is a Document Database?

A document database (also called a NoSQL document store) is a non-relational database that stores data as structured documents. It is a modern way to store data in JSON format rather than simple rows and columns. A document can be a PDF, a document, or an XML or JSON file.

A Document	Key	Value

{
"BookID":"978-1449396091",
"Title":"Redis-The Definitive Guide",
"BookID":"Salvatore Sanfilippo"
"Year":"2021",
}
	BookID	978-1449396091

	Title	Redis - The Definitive Guide
	Author	Salvatore Sanfilippo
	Year	2021

Figure-1.5 Document Database

Querying NoSQL

The question of how to query a NoSQL database is what most developers are interested in. After all, data stored in a huge database doesn't do anyone any good if you can't retrieve and show it to end users or web services. NoSQL databases do not provide a high-level declarative query language like SQL. Instead, querying these databases is data-model specific.

Many of the NoSQL platforms allow for RESTful interfaces to the data. Other offer query APIs. There are a couple of query tools that have been developed that attempt to query multiple NoSQL databases. These tools typically work across a single NoSQL category. One example is SPARQL. SPARQL is a declarative query specification designed for graph databases. Here is an example of an SPARQL query that retrieves the URL of a particular blogger (courtesy of IBM):

```
PREFIX foaf:
SELECT ?url
FROM
WHERE {
?contributor foaf:name "Ajit Singh" .
?contributor foaf:weblog ?url .
}
```

When should NoSQL be used:

1. When huge amount of data need to be stored and retrieved .

2. The relationship between the data you store is not that important

3. The data changing over time and is not structured.

4. Support of Constraints and Joins is not required at database level

5. The data is growing continuously and you need to scale the database regular to handle the data.

Choosing NoSQL database

Given so much choice, how do we choose which NoSQL database? As described much depends on the system requirements, here are some general guidelines:

1. Key-value databases are generally useful for storing session information, user profiles, preferences, shopping cart data. We would avoid using Key-value databases when we need to query by data, have relationships between the data being stored or we need to operate on multiple keys at the same time.

2. Document databases are generally useful for content management systems, blogging platforms, web analytics, real-time analytics, ecommerce-applications. We would avoid using document databases for systems that need complex transactions spanning multiple operations or queries against varying aggregate structures.

3. Column family databases are generally useful for content management systems, blogging platforms, maintaining counters, expiring usage, heavy write volume such as log aggregation. We would avoid using column family databases for systems that are in early development, changing query patterns.

Graph databases are very well suited to problem spaces where we have connected data, such as social networks, spatial data, routing information for goods and money, recommendation engines.

Difference between SQL and NoSQL

When it comes to choosing a database the biggest decisions is picking a relational (SQL) or non-relational (NoSQL) data structure. While both the databases are viable options still there are certain key differences between the two that users must keep in mind when making a decision.

The Main Differences:

1. Type

SQL databases are primarily called as Relational Databases (RDBMS); whereas NoSQL database are primarily called as non-relational or distributed database.

2. Language

SQL databases defines and manipulates data based structured query language (SQL). Seeing from a side this language is extremely powerful. SQL is one of the most versatile and widely-used options available which makes it a safe choice especially for great complex queries. But from other side it can be restrictive. SQL requires you to use predefined schemas to determine the structure of your data before you work with it. Also all of your data must follow the same structure. This can require significant up-front preparation which means that a change in the structure would be both difficult and disruptive to your whole system.

A NoSQL database has dynamic schema for unstructured data. Data is stored in many ways which means it can be document-oriented, column-oriented, graph-based or organized as a KeyValue store. This flexibility means that documents can be created without having defined structure first. Also each document can have its own unique structure. The syntax varies from database to database, and you can add fields as you go.

3. The Scalability

In almost all situations SQL databases are vertically scalable. This means that you can increase the load on a single server by increasing things like RAM, CPU or SSD. But on the other hand NoSQL databases are horizontally scalable. This means that you handle more traffic by sharding, or adding more servers in your NoSQL database. It is similar to adding more floors to the same building versus adding more buildings to the neighborhood. Thus NoSQL can ultimately become larger and more powerful, making these databases the preferred choice for large or ever-changing data sets.

4. The Structure

SQL databases are table-based on the other hand NoSQL databases are either key-value pairs, document-based, graph databases or wide-column stores. This makes relational SQL databases a better option for applications that require multi-row transactions such as an accounting system or for legacy systems that were built for a relational structure.

5. Property followed

SQL databases follow ACID properties (Atomicity, Consistency, Isolation and Durability) whereas the NoSQL database follows the Brewers CAP theorem (Consistency, Availability and Partition tolerance).

6. Support

Great support is available for all SQL database from their vendors. Also a lot of independent consultations are there who can help you with SQL database for a very large scale deployments but for some NoSQL database you still have to rely on community support and only limited outside experts are available for setting up and deploying your large scale NoSQL deployments.

Some examples of SQL databases include PostgreSQL, MySQL, Oracle and Microsoft SQL Server. NoSQL database examples include Redis, RavenDB Cassandra, MongoDB, BigTable, HBase, Neo4j and CouchDB.

SQL vs. NoSQL: Comparison Table

DBMS	SQL databases	NoSQL databases
Type	Relational database	Non-relational database
Structure	SQL databases organize and store data by table and fixed columns and rows	NoSQL databases can be key-value, document column-oriented, and graph
Schema	Fixed schema	Dynamic schema
Scalability	Vertical scalability	Horizontal and vertical scalability
Query	Structured Query Language (SQL)	No declarative query language; it depends on the database type

Figure-1.6

Query Mechanism tools for NoSQL

The most common data retrieval mechanism is the REST-based retrieval of a value based on its key/ID with GET resource

Document store Database offers more difficult queries as they understand the value in a key-value pair. For example, CouchDB allows defining views with MapReduce.

Data Modeling in a NoSQL Database

All businesses have a knack for adding new demands and features to their applications after deployment. Such requirement changes are not just feature requests but entire changes in business process as well. Innovation in any industry is not just a buzzword anymore, it's a necessity, and competition demands rapid adaptability to new requirements.

NoSQL is built to support exactly such fast moving requirements whereas a relational database is inherently slow to such changes due to its rigid data structure. NoSQL databases fully support agile development.

NoSQL Data Model

NoSQL or 'Not Only SQL' is a data model that starkly differs from traditional SQL expectations.

The primary difference is that NoSQL does not use a relational data modeling technique and it emphasizes flexible design. The lack of requirement for a schema makes designing a much simpler and cheaper process. That isn't to say that you can't use a schema altogether, but rather that schema design is very flexible.

Another useful feature of NoSQL data models is that they are built for high efficiency and speed in terms of creating up to millions of queries a second. This is achieved through having all the data contained within one table, and so JOINS and cross-referencing is not as performance heavy. NoSQL is also unique in that it is horizontally scalable, compared to SQL which is only vertically scalable. With NoSQL you can simply use another shard, which is cheap, rather than buying more hardware, which is not.

Schema Design for NoSQL

Since NoSQL databases don't really have a set structure, development and schema design tends to be focused around the physical data model. That means developing for large, horizontally expansive environments, something that NoSQL excels at. Therefore, the specific quirks and problems that come with scalability are at the forefront.

As such, the first step is to define business requirements, as optimizing data access is a must, and can only be achieved by knowing what the business wants to do with the data. Your schema design should complement the workflows tied to your use case.

There are several ways to select the primary key, and ultimately that depends on the users themselves. That being said, some data might suggest a more efficient schema, especially in terms of how often that data is queried

Schema-less Ramifications

All NoSQL databases claim to be schema-less, which means there is no schema enforced by the database themselves. Databases with strong schemas, such as relational databases, can be migrated by saving each schema change, plus its data migration, in a version-controlled sequence. Schema-less databases still need careful migration due to the implicit schema in any code that accesses the data.

Schema-less databases can use the same migration techniques as databases with strong schemas, in schema-less databases we can also read data in a way that's tolerant to changes in the data's implicit schema and use incremental migration to update data, thus allowing for zero downtime deployments, making them more popular with 24*7 systems.

A NoSQL database stores data in Key Value pairs where the "key" is just a unique identifier and the "value" is a JSON document. The closest similar entity in a relational database is a row. A row in an RDBMS is just a flat data structure where the data is divided into columns. The JSON format however, is much, much richer than just a flat data structure. For comparison reasons, the following diagram speaks volumes.

Figure-1.7

The diagram shows a single row of a user data converted to a JSON document. In it, the column names are converted to keys inside a JSON document and the values are retained as is.

For example, if we are to add new information to the user data, it requires a hit on the whole database (i.e. all the rows of a table) which hurts performance on production servers thereby hurting every other application depending on the servers as well.

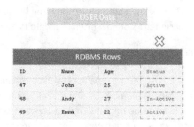

Figure-1.8

NoSQL on the other hand is completely flexible. Instead of defining all the column names before inserting data, a NoSQL database has no data schema restrictions. If your business demands a change or addition in the data from here-forth, no problem. Just add new entities inside new JSON documents.

Figure-1.9

With the help of a NoSQL database, your data schema is flexible and that supports the speed that agile development demands. Your application will accept new changes as required by the business without advanced definition.

NoSQL Data Modeling Techniques

All NoSQL data modeling techniques are grouped into three major groups:

- **Conceptual techniques**
- **General modeling techniques**
- **Hierarchy modeling techniques**

Below, we will briefly discuss all NoSQL data modeling techniques.

Conceptual Techniques

There are a three conceptual techniques for NoSQL data modeling:

1. Denormalization.

Denormalization is a pretty common technique and entails copying the data into multiple tables or forms in order to simplify them. With denormalization, easily group all the data that needs to be queried in one place. Of course, this does mean that data volume does increase for different parameters, which increases the data volume considerably.

2. Aggregates.

This allows users to form nested entities with complex internal structures, as well as vary their particular structure. Ultimately, aggregation reduces joins by minimizing one-to-one relationships. Most NoSQL data models have some form of this soft schema technique. For example, graph and key-value store databases have values that can be of any format, since those data models do not place constraints on value. Similarly, another example such as BigTable has aggregation through columns and column families.

3. Application Side Joins.

NoSQL doesn't usually support joins, since NoSQL databases are question-oriented where joins are done during design time. This is compared to relational databases where are performed at query execution time. Of course, this tends to result in a performance penalty and is sometimes unavoidable.

General Modeling Techniques

There are a five general techniques for NoSQL data modeling:

1. Enumerable Keys.

For the most part, unordered key values are very useful, since entries can be partitioned over several dedicated servers by just hashing the key. Even so, adding some form of sorting functionality through ordered keys is useful, even though it may add a bit more complexity and a performance hit.

2. Dimensionality Reduction.

Geographic information systems tend to use R-Tree indexes and need to be updated in-place, which can be expensive if dealing with large data volumes. Another traditional approach is to flatten the 2D structure into a plain list, such as what is done with Geohash. With dimensionality reduction, you can map multidimensional data to a simple key-value or even non-multidimensional models. Use dimensionality reduction to map multidimensional data to a Key-Value model or to another non-multidimensional model.

3. Index Table.

With an index table, take advantage of indexes in stores that don't necessarily support them internally. Aim to create and then maintain a unique table with keys that follow a specific access pattern. For example, a master table to store user accounts for access by user ID.

4. Composite Key Index.

While somewhat of a generic technique, composite keys are incredibly useful when ordered keys are used. If you take it and combine it with secondary keys, you can create a multidimensional index that is pretty similar to the above-mentioned Dimensionality Reduction technique.

5. Inverted Search.

Direct Aggregation. The concept behind this technique is to use an index that meets a specific set of criteria, but then aggregate that data with full scans or some form of original representation. This is more of a data processing pattern than data modeling, yet data models are certainly affected by using this type of processing pattern. Take into account that random retrieval of records required for this technique is inefficient. Use query processing in batches to mitigate this problem.

Hierarchy Modeling Techniques

There are a seven hierarchy modeling techniques for NoSQL data:

1. Tree Aggregation.

Tree aggregation is essentially modeling data as a single document. This can be really efficient when it comes to any record that is always accessed at once, such as a Twitter thread or Reddit post. Of course, the problem then becomes that random access to any individual entry is inefficient.

2. Adjacency Lists.

This is a straightforward technique where nodes are modeled as independent records of arrays with direct ancestors. That's a complicated way of saying that it allows you to search nodes by their parents or children. Much like tree aggregation though, it is also quite inefficient for retrieving an entire subtree for any given node.

3. Materialized Paths.

This technique is a sort of denormalization and is used to avoid recursive traversals in tree structures. Mainly, we want to attribute the parents or children to each node, which helps us determine any predecessors or descendants of the node without worrying about traversal. Incidentally, we can store materialized paths as IDs, either as a set or a single string.

4. Nested Sets.

A standard technique for tree-like structures in relational databases, it's just as applicable to NoSQL and key-value or document databases. The goal is to store the tree leaves as an array and then map each non-leaf node to a range of leaves using start/end indexes. Modeling it in this way is an efficient way to deal with immutable data as it only requires a small amount of memory, and doesn't necessarily have to use traversals. That being said, updates are expensive because they require updates of indexes.

5. Nested Documents Flattening.

Numbered Field Names. Most search engines tend to work with documents that are a flat list of fields and values, rather than something with a complex internal structure.

As such, this data modeling technique tries to map these complex structures to a plain document, for example, mapping documents with a hierarchical structure, a common difficulty you might encounter.

Of course, this type of work is pain-staking and not easily scalable, especially as the nested structures increase.

6. Nested Documents Flattening.

Proximity Queries. One way to solve the potential problems with the Numbered Field Names data modeling technique is to use a similar technique called Proximity Queries. These limit the distance between words in a document, which helps increase performance and decrease query speed impact.

7. Batch Graph Processing.

Batch graph processing is a great technique for exploring the relationships up or down for a node, within a few steps. It is an expensive process and doesn't necessarily scale very well. By using Message Passing and MapReduce we can carry out this type of graph processing.

Options for Implementing NoSQL

From a practical perspective, how do you go about actually moving to NoSQL and implementing your first application? In general, there are three ways to approach your adoption of a NoSQL database:

1. New applications

Many begin with NoSQL by applying it in new cloud applications and starting from the ground up. This approach avoids the pain of application rewrites and data migrations.

2. Augmentation

Some choose to augment an existing system by adding a NoSQL component to it. This often happens with applications that have outgrown an RDBMS due to scale problems or the need for better availability.

3. Full rip-replace

For systems that exhibit growing costs, or are breaking in major ways due to increased user concurrency, data velocity, or data volume, a full replacement is done with a NoSQL database.

Best Use Cases for NoSQL Databases

1. Key-value store databases

These databases are best used for various shopping carts. This is simply because Key-Value databases can handle millions or billions of orders. Massive incoming data is processed without performance loss. These databases also have built-in redundancy so you won't have to worry about data loss.

2. Document store databases

These databases are best used for various catalogs. This can again be connected to your e-commerce business, where you need to store thousands of different attributes about our products. Since data is stored in a single document, the management of products is fast and easy.

3. Wide-Column Stores

These databases are best used for geographic information, reporting systems, sensor logs, and such. We state this because Wide-Column stores use multi-dimensional mapping (row-value, column-value, and timestamp) in a tabular format meant for massive scalability. If you ever use a website or app to check the driving distance from A to B on a map, chances are pretty high that Wide-Column stores are in use on that website or application.

4. Graph store databases

These databases are best used for above-average fraud detection systems. Let's say that we have a known fraud case on file for a specific email or credit card in question. If that person tries to log in and purchases something again with the information from that fraud case, someone would be notified by the system. That happens because of how the Graph store databases process relationships between nodes in real-time.

Applications of NoSQL Databases

Data Mining

When it comes to data mining, NoSQL databases are useful in retrieving information for data mining uses. Particularly when it's about large amounts of data, NoSQL databases store data points in both structured and unstructured formats leading to efficient storage of big data. Perhaps when a user wishes to mine a particular dataset from large amounts of data, one can make use of NoSQL databases, to begin with. Data is the building block of technology that has led mankind to such great heights. Therefore, one of the most essential fields where NoSQL databases can be put to use is data mining and data storage.

Social Media Networking Sites

Social media is full of data, both structured and unstructured. A field that is loaded with tons of data to be discovered, social media is one of the most effective applications of NoSQL databases.

From comments to posts, user-related information to advertising, social media marketing requires NoSQL databases to be implemented in certain ways to retrieve useful information that can be helpful in certain ways.

Social media sites like Facebook and Instagram often approach open-source NoSQL databases to extract data that helps them keep track of their users and the activities going on around their platforms.

Software Development

The third application that we will be looking at is software development. Software development requires extensive research on users and the needs of the masses that are met through software development.

However, a developer must be able to scan through data that is available. Perhaps NoSQL databases are always useful in helping software developers keep a tab on their users, their details, and other user-related data that is important to be noted. That said, NoSQL databases are surely helpful in software development.

Major NoSQL Players

The major players in NoSQL have emerged primarily because of the organizations that have adopted them. Some of the largest NoSQL technologies include:

- Dynamo: Dynamo was created by Amazon.com and is the most prominent Key-Value NoSQL database. Amazon was in need of a highly scalable distributed platform for their e-commerce businesses so they developed Dynamo. Amazon S3 uses Dynamo as the storage mechanism.
- Cassandra: Cassandra was open sourced by Facebook and is a column-oriented NoSQL database.
- BigTable: BigTable is Google's proprietary column oriented database. Google allows the use of BigTable but only for the Google App Engine.
- SimpleDB: SimpleDB is another Amazon database. Used for Amazon EC2 and S3, it is part of Amazon Web Services that charges fees depending on usage.
- CouchDB: CouchDB along with MongoDB are open source document-oriented NoSQL databases.
- Neo4J: Neo4j is an open source graph database.

Chapter 2
NoSQL Concepts

This chapter describes the state of the art regarding the field of non-relational databases. It reviews the theoretical background and recent breakthroughs, detailing background knowledge that is integrated into the technologies, which is required in order to fully understand the domain of non-relation databases.

CAP Theorem

The CAP theorem (also known as Brewer's theorem), is a theorem on distributed systems which states that of the following desired properties in a distributed system: Consistency, Availability and Partition-tolerance; it is impossible to achieve all of the three properties at the same time. Therefore, at most only two of these properties can be satisfied.

The theorem was introduced in 2000 at the Symposium on Principles of Distributed Comput-ing by computer scientist Eric Brewer as a conjecture and was formally proved in 2002 by Seth Gilbert and Nancy Lynch, therefore establishing it as a theorem.

The CAP theorem has implications on the design of distributed systems and must be taken into account. Since most NoSQL databases are distributed systems it plays an important role on this field. In the context of NoSQL, it is important to understand the different properties of the CAP theorem, as different databases seem to satisfy different properties.

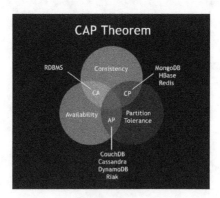

Figure-2.0

Consistency

In the context of distributed systems, consistency means that all the nodes of the system see the same data at the same time. Therefore, the system guarantees that once you store a given state, the system will book that same state in every subsequent operation (on every node of the system), until it is explicitly changed. Full consistency is easier to achieve in a non-distributed environment and it is usually supported by most of the RDBMS that comply with ACID (discussed later). On the other hand, it is a lot harder to achieve in a distributed environment, and sometimes it may not even be desirable, since the overall performance of the system may drop as the number of nodes increases. It is necessary to resort to network communication between nodes to make sure they all share the same data. Most often, distributed systems may provide a form of weak consistency which will be discussed later on this chapter.

Availability

Availability means that the system is ensured to remain operational over a period of time (it is therefore a probabilistic metric). In this context, it represents a system on which node failures do not prevent survivors from continuing to operate. One of the main reasons to distribute a system is to provide high availability, as more nodes are part of the system and share some data, the system becomes more tolerant to particular node failures. A centralized system cannot provide high availability given that if the only node of the system fails, the system is no longer able to operate.

Partition Tolerance

Partition Tolerance implies that a system must continue to operate despite arbitrary message loss between the different nodes of the distributed system.

The constituent nodes of a distributed system are required to communicate with each other, sharing data and state to ensure the system is operational and provides some form of consistency. In the presence of a network failure, some of the nodes of the system may no longer be able to communicate and the system becomes partitioned. If the system is partition tolerant then it must be able to perform as usual, despite the temporary partition.

In the case of a distributed database if it is partition tolerant then it will still be able to perform read/write operations while partitioned. If it is not partition tolerant, when partitioned, the database may become completely unusable or only available for read operations.

ACID vs. BASE

Distributed systems, and databases in particular, usually offer a defined consistency model. These models guarantee that if certain conditions are met we can expect different properties to be assured (i.e. consistency, availability, partition tolerance).

In this section, the popular ACID set of properties that guarantee database transactions are processed reliably, is compared to the opposing BASE model, which is derived directly from the CAP theorem, but aims to provide a different set of properties than ACID does.

ACID

Traditionally, relational databases are able to provide and comply with the ACID properties, which is a set of properties that guarantee database transactions are processed reliably and that the database is consistent in the face of concurrent accesses and system failure. ACID is an acronym which means the following: Atomicity, Consistency, Isolation and Durability.

Atomicity: Atomicity means that database transactions must follow an "all or nothing" rule. Given that a transaction is a series of instructions to be executed (as one), for the transaction to be "atomic", all the instructions must be executed, or if one (or more) fail, the entire transaction should fail, and the database should remain unchanged.

Consistency: Consistency ensures only valid data is written to the database, guaranteeing that if a transaction is executed successfully the database is taken from a consistent state to a new consistent state. If for any reason, an error occurs during the transaction, then any changes already made will be automatically rolled back, therefore ensuring that the database remains in a consistent state.

Isolation: Isolation requires that a transaction in process and not yet committed must remain isolated from any other transaction, therefore the execution of a transaction must not impact the execution of other concurrent transactions. Isolation is important because, as transactions are being executed, the state of the system may not be consistent, since transactions only ensure that the system remains consistent after the transaction ends. If a transaction was not running in isolation, it would be able to access data from the system that may not be consistent.

Durability: Durability ensures that any transaction committed to the database is permanent and will not be lost. The database system must be able to recover the committed transaction updates against any kind of system failure (hardware or software). Many databases implement durability by writing transactions into a transaction log that can be reprocessed to recreate the system state right before any later failure. A transaction is deemed committed only after it is entered in the log.

The ACID model provides the consistency choice for partitioned databases, it is pessimistic and forces consistency at the end of every operation. This strong consistency may not always be necessary, depending on the requirements of the problem domain. It is also very difficult to im-plement in a distributed system without creating bottlenecks. For example, the two-phase commit protocol is able to provide atomicity for distributed transactions, still it is a blocking pro-tocol, a node will block while it is waiting for a message. It also creates overhead as it involves a great deal of communication.

Also, if we take into account the CAP theorem, if we are getting strict consistency we may be jeopardizing either availability or partition tolerance. If we use a two-phase commit protocol we are able to provide consistency across partitions, therefore losing availability. As different applications may have different consistency (and availability) needs, NoSQL databases tend to provide alternative consistency models.

BASE

BASE, as its name suggests, is the logical opposite of ACID. While ACID focuses more on strong consistency by being pessimistic, BASE takes availability as it's primary objective, it is optimistic and provides eventual consistency. BASE is an acronym standing for Basically Available, Soft-state, Eventual consistency. It is intrinsically connected with the CAP theorem and it was also proposed by Eric Brewer in 2000 at the Symposium on Principles of Distributed Computing.

Eventual Consistency

Eventual Consistency: is a specific form of weak consistency. A distributed system that provides eventual consistency guarantees that given that no new updates are made to a record, eventually the system will be consistent (i.e. all the nodes of the system will "eventually" hold the same values, although that may not be necessary for example when using quorums), and all read accesses will return the latest updated value.

The period between the update and the moment that it is guaranteed that the system is consistent is called the inconsistency window. The maximum size of this inconsistency window can be determined based on a number of factors such as, system load and number of replicas. There are different variations on the eventual consistency model that we might consider.

Causal consistency: If a certain process communicates to another process that it has updated a value, a subsequent access by that process will return the updated value, and a write is guaranteed to supersede the earlier write. Access by another distinct process that has no causal relationship to the originator process is subject to the normal eventual consistency rules.

Read Your Writes consistency: The effect of a write operation by a process on a variable is always seen in a subsequent read operation of the same variable by the same process.

Session consistency: A variation of read your writes, which assures that a process is able to read it's own writes during a specific session. Out of the context of that session the same process might see older values.

Monotonic reads: If a process reads the value of a variable, any subsequent reading of that variable by the same process should return the same value or a more up-to-date value.

Monotonic writes: A write operation of a variable by a process completes before the following write operation of the same variable by the same process. The system guarantees to serialize writes performed by the same process.

Taking into account the CAP theorem, eventual consistency plays an important role on NoSQL databases because it gives the database the ability to relax consistency, effectively trading it for availability (or partition tolerance).

Multiversion Concurrency Control

Multi-version concurrency control (MVCC) is a concurrency control mechanism that enables con-current access to a certain resource (e.g. a database). It was first described in a 1978 text by David Reed and since then it has been implemented widely on relational databases, such as, PostgreSQL, MySQL and also on some NoSQL databases, such as, CouchDB.

Multiversion concurrency control is an alternative to locking and it is able to provide efficient parallel access to data avoiding the possibility of data corruption and deadlocks. Locking works by giving exclusive access to a certain record to a requesting process. Until that process releases the lock, any other processes trying to access that record (even for reading) have to wait. This model effectively serializes the requests and grants exclusive access to requesting parties. It can be seen as a pessimistic stance on concurrency.

In MVCC instead of granting exclusive access to a resource, the resources are versioned, and whenever processes request access they are given a copy of the latest version available. This way, processes are able to read data in parallel, even if another process is writing to this resource. Therefore, MVCC takes a more optimistic stance on concurrency.

To achieve consistency, each data item has attached to it a timestamp (or a revision number). Whenever a process reads a resource, it retrieves its value as well as this timestamp. If that same process wants to update this record, whenever it tries to write to the database the new value is sent as well as the original timestamp. If the latest revision's timestamp is the same, then this new value is written and the timestamp is updated, effectively creating a modified copy of the original data. If the timestamp is not the same, then it means that another process already updated the record in the meantime, which means that our changes were not made on the latest version, generating a conflict.

The database may deal with this conflict by requesting the conflicting client to re-read the record (with the new value) and redo the update operation. Some databases might instead store all the conflicting revisions of a certain record and let the client solve the conflict by himself. The client might then chose one version, or merge both.

On some database systems (e.g. CouchDB) MVCC also allows to perform disk access opti-mizations. Since updates mean that a new copy of the data item is completely recreated it allows to write entire data items onto contiguous sections of a disk. Although this technique offers some advantages over locking, it comes with the drawback of having to store multiple versions of data items, therefore increasing the database's size.

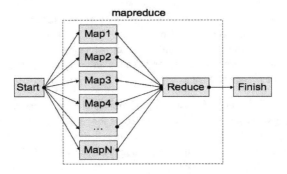

Figure 2.1: MapReduce job representation

MapReduce

MapReduce is a programming model and an associated implementation for processing and gener-ating large data sets. It was developed by Google to support their indexing system.

Given a big data set, it may be necessary to process it and perform certain operations on it. The data set may be big enough that computing power of a single machine may not suffice and it may be necessary to distribute the task across several machines. By using the MapReduce frame-work a developer is able to write applications that are automatically distributed across multiple computers without him having to deal with issues such as parallelization, synchronization and distribution. As the name implies, MapReduce is a two-step process: map and reduce.

"Map" step The master node takes the input, chops it up into smaller sub-problems, and dis-tributes those to worker nodes. A worker node may do this again in turn, leading to a multi-level tree structure. The worker node processes that smaller problem, and passes the answer back to its master node.

"Reduce" step The master node then takes the answers to all the sub-problems and combines them in some way to get the output – the answer to the problem it was originally trying to solve.

In Figure 2.1 a representation of the MapReduce phases and work distribution is pre-sented. To be able to use the MapReduce framework, a user must simply provide the appropriate map and reduce functions that are to be used in each of these steps. The map function takes an input

```
1  map(String key, String value):

2    // key: document name

3    // value: document contents

4    for each word w in value:

5      EmitIntermediate(w, "1");

6  reduce(String key, Iterator values):

7    // key: a word

8    // values: a list of counts

9    int result = 0;

10   for each v in values:

11     result += ParseInt(v);

12   Emit(AsString(result))
```

Listing 2.1: Example map and reduce functions for word counting

pair and produces a set of intermediate key/value pairs. The reduce function accepts an intermedi-ate key and a set of values for that key. It merges together these values to form a possibly smaller set of values, typically just zero or one output value is produced per reduce invocation.

Example

The MapReduce paper published by Google presents a simple example on the usage of the MapRe-duce framework that helps understanding the key concepts.

Considering we want to count the number of occurrences of each word in a very large set of documents, it may be useful to rely on the MapReduce technique to distribute the task. To do so, we must specify map and reduce functions.

The map function emits a key/value pair for each word found in a certain document. The key represents the word and the value represents the number of occurrences (1 in this case).

The reduce function sums together all counts (value) emitted for a particular word (key) and emits the final result.

Pseudo-code for this example is presented in Listing 2.1.

Relationship to NoSQL

Although MapReduce was first implemented, as proprietary software, by Google, there are now free implementations like Apache Hadoop. It is also widely available and used in many NoSQL databases.

As NoSQL databases tend to be distributed and usually deal with very large data sets, batch processing of data and aggregation operations (SQL's COUNT, SUM, etc.) are usually imple-mented as MapReduce operations, so as to be able to evenly distribute the work across the system, while providing an easy framework for the developer to deal with.

Hinted Handoff

Hinted handoff is a mechanism developed by Amazon to use on Dynamo, their highly-available key-value store. This mechanism attempts to increase system availability in the case of node failures. Let us consider the following scenario: a write request is sent to the database, but the node responsible to perform the write operation (i.e. the owner of that record) is not available, either due to a network partition or system failure. In order to allow the write operation to be successful, it is redirected to another node where a hint is attached, i.e. this node records the operation but notes (hints) that it is not the owner of that record and therefore should replay the operation on the node that owns that record when it comes back online.

By using hinted handoff, the database ensures that the read and write operations are not failed due to temporary node or network failures.

Chapter 3
NoSQL Technologies

The number of available non-relational databases is relatively large and is constantly increasing. In this chapter some of the available NoSQL technologies are presented. These databases were chosen based on their maturity, relevance and applicability to the case study that will be developed as part of this project.

For each database their data model, query model, replication model and consistency model is analyzed.

Additionally, for some of the databases a case study is presented detailing the related worked performed with such databases. The presented case studies are fairly brief and do not go into much detail mainly because there is a lack of information to support them.

CouchDB

Apache CouchDB is a free and open-source document-oriented database. It is a top-level project of the Apache Foundation and it is written in Erlang, a programming language aimed at concurrent and distributed applications. It complies with the ACID properties, providing serialized updates and with the use of MVCC reads are never locked.

It is distributed in nature and supports various types of replication schemes and conflict reso-lution.

Data Model

CouchDB stores data in semi-structured documents. A document is a JSON file which is a collec-tion of named key-value pairs. Values can either be numbers, string, booleans, lists or dictionaries. The documents are completely schema-free and do not have to follow any structure (except for JSON's inherent structure).

An example document is shown in Listing 3.1, this document models the information neces-sary do describe a book. Each document in a CouchDB database is identified by a unique ID (the

```
1 {
2   "_id":"282e1890a8095bcc0cb1318bed85bcb377e2700f",
3   "_rev":"946B7D1C",
4   "Type":"Book"
5   "Title":"Flatland",
6   "Author":"Edwin A. Abbot",
7   "Date":"2009-10-09",
8   "Language":"English",
9   "ISBN":"1449548660",
10  "Tags":["flatland", "mathematics", "geometry"],
11 }
```

Listing 3.1: Example of a CouchDB document

"_id" field). CouchDB is a simple container of a collection of documents and it does not establish any mandatory relationship between them.

Views Although CouchDB does not enforce any kind of relationship between documents it is usually desirable to have some kind of structure on how the documents are organized. To do so, CouchDB provides a view model.

Views are methods to aggregate and book existing documents on the database. They do not affect the underlying existing data on the base, they simply change the way data is represented, and define the application's design.

To define a view the user must provide a JavaScript function that acts as the "map" function of a MapReduce operation. This function takes a document as argument and it is able to manipulate the document's data in any way desired. The resulting view is a document that might have multiple rows. Let's imagine the case were we have a document collection of books (similar in structure to the one presented in Listing 3.1). We might be interested in getting the title of all the books currently stored in the database, to do so we create the corresponding "map" function to be used in a view, as seen in Listing 3.2.

Views can also have a "reduce" function, which is used to produce aggregate results for a given view.

As views can be computationally complex to generate, CouchDB provides the facility to index views. Instead of constantly recreating views from scratch, CouchDB indexes views and updates

```
1 function(doc) {

2    if (doc.Type == "Book") {

3        emit(null, {Title: doc.Title};

4    }

5 }
```

Listing 3.2: Example map function to create a book title view them incrementally as the databases' data changes.

Query Model

CouchDB exposes a RESTful HTTP API to perform basic CRUD operations on all stored items and it uses the HTTP methods POST, GET, PUT and DELETE to do so. More complex queries can be implemented in the form of views (as was seen before) and the result of these views can also be read using the REST API.

Replication Model

CouchDB is a peer-based distributed database system, it allows peers to update and change data and then bi-directionally synchronize the changes. Therefore, we can model ei-ther master-slave setups (were synchronizations are unidirectional) or master-master setups were changes can happen in either of the nodes and they must be synchronized in a bidirectional way. In order to do so, CouchDB employs optimistic replication, and it has the ability to handle conflicts, that might happen when replicating changes.

For conflict handling, CouchDB relies on the MVCC model. Each document is assigned a revision id and every time a document is updated, the old version is kept and the updated version is given a different revision id. Whenever a conflict is detected, the winning version is saved as the most recent version and the losing version is also saved in the document's history.

This is done consistently throughout all the nodes so that the exact same choices are made. The application can then chose to handle the conflict by itself (ignoring one version or merging the changes).

Consistency Model

CouchDB provides eventual consistency. As multiple masters are allowed, changes need to be propagated to the remaining nodes, and the database does not lock on writes. Therefore, until the changes are propagated from node to node the database remains in a inconsistent state. Still, single master setups (with multiple slaves) are also supported, and in this case strong consistency can be achieved.

Usage at CERN

The European Organization for Nuclear Research (CERN), makes use of CouchDB in order to collect the data captured by the Compact Muon Solenoid (CMS), a general purpose detector that is part of the Large Hadron Collider (LHC).

The data generated must be collected for offline processing and that involves cataloguing data and transferring it across different computing centers for distributed computing. When the LHC is running at it's full power, the CMS alone will collect roughly 10PB of data per year. Being able to easily access and consolidate data from distributed locations with minimal la-tency is required routinely, and was one of the main reasons CouchDB was chosen, for it's ability to perform on a distributed environment with a multi-master setup.

Another reason for its use was the ability to quickly prototype and adapt the system. The team often doesn't have clearly defined requirements and needs to quickly create a new part of the system and deploy it right away. With CouchDB being schema-free and not enforcing any kind of relationship between data, it is a perfect fit to achieve a higher speed of development.

MongoDB

MongoDB (from "humongous") is a free and open-source document-oriented database written in C++. Aside from the open-source community, the development is also supported by the company 10gen.

It is completely schema-free and manages JSON-style documents, as in CouchDB. It focuses on high-performance and agile development, providing the developer with a set of features to easily model and query data, as well as to scale the system.

Data Model

MongoDB stores data as BSON objects, which is a binary-encoded serialization of JSON-like documents. It supports all the data types that are part of JSON but also defines new data types, i.e. the Date data type and the BinData type. The key advantage of using BSON is efficiency (both in space and compute time), as it is a binary format.

Documents are contained in "collections", they can be seen as an equivalent to relational database tables. Collections can contain any kind of document, no relationship is en-forced, still documents within a collection usually have the same structure as it provides a logical way to organize data.

As data within a collections is usually contiguous on disk, if collections are smaller better performance is achieved.

Each document is identified by a unique ID ("_id" field), which can be given by the user upon document creating or automatically generated by the database. An index is automati-cally created on the ID field although other indexes can be manually created in order to speed up common queries.

Relationships can be modeled in two different ways embedding documents or referencing documents. Embedding documents means that a document might contain other data fields related to the document, i.e. a document modeling a blog post would also contain the post's comments. This option might lead to denormalization of the database, as the same data might be embedded in different documents. Referencing documents can be seen as the relational database equivalent of using a foreign-key. Instead of embedding the whole data, the document might instead store the ID of the foreign document so that it can fetched. It is important to note that MongoDB does not

1 db.books.find({'title': 'Flatland'})

Listing 3.3: Example query for finding all books titled "Flatland"

provide the ability to join documents, therefore when referencing documents, any necessary join has to be done on the client-side.

Query Model

MongoDB supports dynamic (ad hoc) queries over all documents inside a collection (including embedded documents). Many traditional SQL queries have a similar counterpart on Mongo's Query Language. Queries are expressed as JSON objects and are sent to MongoDB by the database driver (typically using the "find" method).

In Listing 3.3, we see a simple example were we query the database for all the books with the title 'Flatland'. In addition to exact matching fields, MongoDB also supports regular expressions, comparators, conditional operators and logical operators.

Sorting and counting features are also provided as can be seen in Listing 3.4, the first query retrieves all the books that are written in English sorting them by their title. The second query retrieves the number of books written in English.

More complex queries can be expressed using a MapReduce operation, and it may be useful for batch processing of data and aggregation operations. The user specifies the map and reduce functions in JavaScript and they are executed on the server side. The results of the operation are stored in a temporary collection which is automatically removed after the client gets the results. It is also possible for the results to be stored in a permanent collection, so that they are always available.

Replication Model

MongoDB provides Master-Slave replication and Replica sets, where data is asynchronously repli-cated between servers. In either case only one server is used for write operations at a given time, while read operations can be redirected to slave servers.

Replica sets are an extension of the popular Master-Slave replication scheme in order to pro-vide automatic failover and automatic recovery of member nodes. A replicate set is a group of servers where at any point in time there is only one master server, but the set is able to

```
1 db.books.find({'language': 'English'}).sort({'title':1})

2 db.books.find({'language': 'English'}).count()
```

Listing 3.4: Example queries using aggregation operators

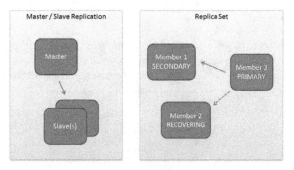

Figure 3.1: Illustration of master-slave replication and replica sets

Select a new master if the current one goes down. Data is replicated among all the servers from the set. Figure 3.1 illustrates the two different replication models.

Consistency Model

Since MongoDB has only one single active master at any point in time, strong consistency can be achieved if all the read operations are done on the master.

Since replication to the slave servers is done asynchronously and MongoDB does not provide version concurrency control, reads from the slave servers employ eventual consistency semantics.

The ability to read from slave servers is usually desired to achieve load balance, therefore the client is also able to enforce that a certain write has replicated to a certain number of slave servers. This feature helps dealing with important writes, where eventual consistency semantics might not be suitable, while at the same time providing the flexibility to read from slave servers.

Cassandra

Apache Cassandra is a free and open-source distributed, structured key-value store with eventual consistency. It is a top-level project of the Apache Foundation and it was initially developed by Facebook. It is designed to handle very large amounts of data, while providing high availability and scalability.

Data Model

Cassandra follows a key-value model, although the value is an object that is highly structured and that contains multiple dimensions. The various dimensions that form Cassandra's data model are presented below.

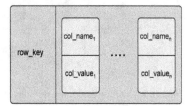

Figure 3.2: Cassandra column

Column The column (Figure 3.2) is the smallest entity of data, and it is a tuple that contains a name and a value. A timestamp is also present, that is used for conflict resolution. A column can be interpreted as a record in a relational database.

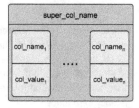

Figure 3.3: Cassandra super column

Super Column A supercolumn (Figure 3.3) can be seen as a column that itself has subcolumns. Similarly to a column, it is a tuple that contains a name and a value, although the value in this case is a map[1] containing columns.

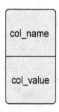

Figure 3.4: Cassandra column family

Column Family A column family (Figure 3.4) contains an infinite number of rows. Each row has a key and a map of columns, sorted by their names. It can be interpreted has a table in

1 insert(table, key, rowMutation)

2 get(table, key, columnName)

3 delete(table, key, columnName)

Listing 3.5: Data access methods of Cassandra

a relational database, although no schema is enforced, a row does not have a predefined list of columns that it contains.

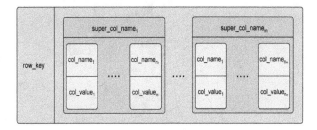

Figure 3.5: Cassandra super column family

Super Column Family Similarly to Column Families, a Super Column Family Figure 3.5) is a container for Super Columns.

Keyspace A keyspace is a collection of Column Families. It usually groups all the data related to an application. They can be interpreted as a schema or database in a relational database.

Query Model

Since Cassandra is in essence a key-value store, the querying model provides only three simple operations, as seen in Listing 3.5.

All the accesses are done by key and return the column value associated with that key. Addi-tional methods for getting multiple values or getting multiple columns are also available, but they all rely on the key as input.

Additionally it is also possible to run MapReduce jobs on the database, in order to process complex queries. This can be done by using Apache Hadoop which is a framework for distributed data processing. In order to simplify this task, Cassandra also provides Pig support, which enables the user to write complex MapReduce jobs in a high-level language similar to SQL.

It's important to note that these queries aren't usually supposed to be answered in real-time, they are mainly used as an off-line method of data analysis.

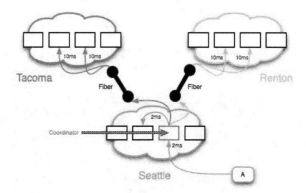

Figure 3.6: Cassandra's replication example between different datacenters

Replication Model

As Cassandra is distributed in nature, data is partitioned over a set of nodes and each data item is assigned to a specific node.

Data items are assigned a position by hashing the data item's key, using consistent hashing. Nodes are also assigned a random value within the hashing's space, which rep-resents it's position on the ring. To find which node is the coordinator for a given data item, it is necessary to go through the ring in a clockwise manner, and find the first node with a position larger than the data item's position.

The client is able to specify the number of replicas that each data item should have. The data item's coordinator node is then responsible for the replication. Several replication policies are available, were the system might be aware of a node's geographic position (i.e. replicate to other datacenters or to other racks).

In Figure 3.6 , we can see a simple replication example. The value A was written to the coordinator node, which then replicated the changes to two additional nodes. One of the replication nodes was in the same datacenter, and the other two were on another datacenter. Using this replication model, Cassandra provides durability guarantees in the presence of node failures or network partitions.

Consistency Model

Cassandra uses a configurable quorum-based approach. The client is able to specify consistency levels per query, which enables it to manage the trade-off of availability vs. con-sistency.

The consistency levels for write operations are as follow:

Any – Ensure that the write is done on at least one node;

One – Ensure that the write has been replicated to at least one node;

Quorum – Ensure that the write has been replicated to a quorum of replicas;

Local Quorum – Ensure that the write has been replicated to a quorum of replicas in the same datacenter of the coordinator node;

Each Quorum – Ensure that the write has been replicated to a quorum of replicas in each datacenter of the cluster;

All – Ensure that the write has been replicated to all replicas.

The consistency levels for read operations have similar meanings and are as follow:

One – Reads from the closest replica;

Quorum – Reads the record once a quorum of replicas has booked;

Local Quorum – Reads the record once a quorum of replicas, in the datacenter of the coordinator node has booked;

Each Quorum – Reads the record once a quorum of replicas, in each datacenter of the cluster has booked;

All – Reads the record once all replicas have replied.

Although Cassandra is usually seen as an eventually consistent system, since consistency is highly tunable, the client can opt for strong consistency or eventual consistency.

Usage at Facebook

Facebook is a social network service and website that allows users to create a personal profile, add other users as friends and exchange messages. Facebook uses Cassandra to power it's inbox search feature, providing users with the ability to search through their Facebook inbox. This means that the system is required to handle a very high write throughput, billions of writes per day, and also scale with the number of users. As data is distributed geographically across different data centers it is also necessary to be able to replicate between data centers.

Cassandra was developed by Facebook to address this problem. To do so, a per user index of all messages that have been exchanged between the sender and the recipients of the message is maintained, where the different terms used in the message are stored to easily and efficiently be able to answer a search query.

This feature was deployed initially to around 100 million users which accounted to roughly 7TB of inbox data. The system is now being used widely, storing about 50TB of data on a 150 node cluster, providing high performance and scalability.

Riak

Riak is a free and open-source distributed key-value store inspired by Amazon's Dynamo, imple-menting the principles detailed in Dynamos's paper. Besides the open-source commu-nity its development is also overseen by the company Basho.

It is primarily written in Erlang and C. It is a fault-tolerant with no single point of failure, sup-porting high availability and providing tunable levels of guarantees for durability and consistency.

An enterprise version with added features is also available although it will not be discussed in this document.

Data Model

In Riak data is organized in a simple manner consisting of Buckets, Keys and Values (also referred to as Objects).

Values hold the data to be stored and they can store any kind of data as required by the user wether it be binary data, simple textual data, or a structured document like a JSON object. Values are identified and accessed by a unique key and each key-value pair is stored in a bucket.

It is important to take into account that Riak is content-agnostic, therefore it does not differ-entiate if the value is either a JSON document or a simple string. Therefore, if we, for example, model an object using a JSON document it is impossible to only fetch one of the attributes (sim-ilarly to fetching a column value on a relational database) as Riak doesn't know how to interpret JSON documents.

A bucket is a namespace and provides only a logical separation of data. Although there is no requirement on data structure stored within a bucket, it is usually desirable to store similar data within the same bucket. A bucket can be interpreted as an analogous to a table in a relational database, where similar data is contained.

To complement this fairly simple key-value data model, the concept of links is introduced. Links define one-way relationships between different objects, providing the user with a simple way to create relationships between data. A single object may hold several links pointing to different objects.

Query Model

Riak provides the usual simple methods to access data existing in a key-value store, that is, all the accesses are done by key, providing the ability to add new objects, get existing objects, update objects and delete objects.

These methods can be accessed by using a RESTful HTPP API, where the HTTP methods POST, GET, PUT and DELETE are used respectively to create, read, update and delete objects.

Additionally, a native Erlang interface and a Protocol Buffers interface provide the same utilities.

MapReduce More powerful and complex queries can be issued using MapReduce. The map and reduce functions can be written in either Erlang or

JavaScript and they can be executed using the Erlang API or the REST API, respectively.

Link Walking A powerful feature of Riak is the ability to add links between different objects. Given the existing links, it is possible to follow links from one object to another, effectively travers-ing the chain of connected objects. To do so we can use the existing methods in the API.

Riak Search is a platform built by Basho that runs on top of the Riak key-value store and provides a full-text search engine. The user is then able to retrieve an object given it's value. It may be useful when using Riak as it provides additional access methods. Still, this technology is not discussed in-depth as it is still in an early stage of development.

Replication Model

Since both Riak and Cassandra are based on Amazon's Dynamo they share some characteristics regarding the replications model.

Riak data is also partitioned over a ring of nodes, in the same way Cassandra does. In Figure 3.7 it is possible to see the data distribution and replication across the ring of nodes. Every color represents a physical node responsible for a given range of the keyspace.

Replication properties are configured on a per-bucket basis. The client is able to specify how many replicas of data should be kept, and the system automatically replicates the data within a bucket across the cluster, to match the specified replication factor.

As nodes join or leave the cluster, Riak automatically re-balances the data.

Consistency Model

Similarly to Cassandra, Riak also provides tunable consistency controls, allowing the user to easily adapt the system to different CAP properties.

Riak uses a quorum-based approach that allows the user to specify the number of replicas that must book for a given operation (e.g. write operation) to be considered complete and successful.

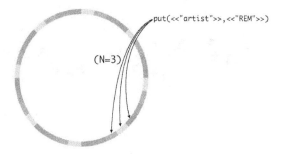

Figure 3.7: Example of data replication with a replication factor of 3

The API allows the user to manually set the number of replicas that must book to an operation, by simply providing the desired value. The user may also use one of the existing symbolic options which are:

All − Requires that all replicas reply;

One − Requires that only one replicas reply;

Quorum − Requires that a majority of the replicas (i.e. quorum) reply.

With this capability the user is able to efficiently control consistency constraints, moving the system from eventually consistent to strongly consistent as needed.

HBase

HBase is a free and open-source distributed, column-oriented database, which is modeled after Google's BigTable and is written in Java.

It is developed as part of Apache Software Foundation's Hadoop project and runs on top of HDFS (Hadoop Distributed Filesystem), providing BigTable-like capabilities for Hadoop, ensuring a fault-tolerant way of storing large quantities of sparse data.

Data Model

HBase's data model is very similar to that of Cassandra, since they are both based on Google's BigTable. It also follows a key-value model where the value is a tuple consisting of a row key, a

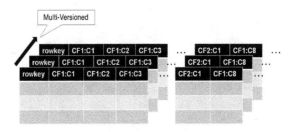

Figure 3.8: Representation of HBase's data model

column key and a timestamp (i.e. a cell). Data is stored into tables, which are made of rows and columns, as seen in Figure 3.8 .

A row consists of a row key and a variable number of columns. Rows are lexicographically sorted with the lowest order appearing first in a table.

Columns contain a version history of their contents, ordered by a timestamp. Columns are grouped into Column Families and they all have a common prefix in the form of family:qualifier. Since tunings and storage specifications are done at the column family level, it is desirable that all column family members have the same general access pattern and size characteristics.

Query Model

HBase provides a Java API that can be used to make queries. The obvious map operations: put, delete and update are provided by this API.

An abstraction layer Filter, gives applications the ability to define several filters for a row key, column families, column key and timestamps and the results can be iterated using the Scanner abstraction.

For more complex queries it is possible to write MapReduce jobs that run on the underlying Hadoop infrastructure. Using Pig it is possible to query data using an high-level, SQL-like, language. It is also possible to use Cascading to simplify the process of writing MapReduce jobs.

In addition to the Java API, it is also possible to access HBase through REST, Avro or Thrift gateway APIs. A shell for direct user interaction with HBase also exists.

Replication Model

HBase uses a simple master-slave replication model. The replication is done asyn-chronously, meaning that the clusters can be geographically distant, the links connecting them can be offline for some time, and rows inserted on the master server may not be available at the same time on the slave servers, therefore providing only eventual consistency.

Replication is performed by replicating whole WALEdits in order to maintain atomicity. WALEd-its are used in HBase's transaction log (WAL) to represent the collection of edits corresponding to a single transaction.

Consistency Model

HBase is strictly consistent, every value appears in one region only, within the appropriate bound-ary for its row key, and each region is assigned to only one region server at a time.

If replication is enabled and one reads from the slave servers, only eventual consistency can be guaranteed, since the replication is done asynchronously.

Row operations are atomic and it is possible to make transactions inside a row. Transactions over multiple rows are not supported at the moment of this writing.

Usage at Google

Google Analytics[3] is a free service offered by Google that generates detailed statistics about the visitors to a website, such as the number of unique visitors per day and the number of page views per URL per day.

Webmasters are required to embed a small JavaScript program in their web pages that is re-sponsible for recording various information about the request in Google Analytics (e.g. user iden-tifier and information about the page being fetched). This raw information is then processed, summarized and presented to the webmaster by Google Analytics.

In order to power the storage and processing of this data, Google relies on BigTable (which is analogous to HBase) and the MapReduce framework. A table that stores raw clicks (which is around 200TB) maintains a row for each end-user session. This row is identified by the website's name and the time at which the session was created, making sure that sessions for the same website are stored contiguously and sorted chronologically.

An additional summary table contains the various predefined summaries for each website, which were generated by running a MapReduce job over the raw click table.

CAP Properties

This section attempts to compare the CAP properties: consistency, availability and partition toler-ance of each of the described databases with each other. Figure 3.9 shows the relative distribution of the databases according to these three properties.

Traditional Relational Database Management System (RDBMS) are known for their ability to provide strong consistency. At a transaction-level this consistency is usually supported by the ACID set of properties. Taking into consideration a distributed RDBMS (with a master-slave

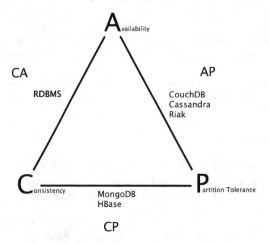

Figure 3.9: Classification of databases according to CAP theorem

configuration) it is also able to provide availability, still, it is only able to deliver it when there is connectivity between the different RDBMS nodes; if there is a partition between these entities (i.e. the master and slaves) the system is not able to properly function. Therefore, it can be said that the RDBMS does not provide partition tolerance.

Available and partition tolerant databases, such as CouchDB, Cassandra and Riak, usually relax consistency restraints by providing "eventual consistency". All of these databases support asynchronous replication yielding high degrees of availability. Mechanisms such as hinted handoff also allow the system to achieve partition tolerance. It's important to keep in mind that both Riak and Cassandra allow the user to vary the desired consistency level at a query-level, therefore being able to trade-off some availability for consistency.

Finally, both MongoDB and HBase provide consistency and partition tolerance. Both HBase and MongoDB provide a strict consistency model across partitioned nodes, which sacrifices avail-ability.

Conclusions

Although this technology review only addressed five NoSQL databases, it is possible to notice that there are a lot of differences among them. Different databases rely on different design principles in an effort to provide certain properties.

Throughout the rest of this work, the study will be focused on Riak and Cassandra. This two databases were chosen because they provide distinct data models which will allow for a wider research on data modeling techniques. They also both provide easy and flexible scalability (i.e. horizontal scalability) as well as high availability. Another important aspect is that both these databases allow for the definition of consistency constraints on an operation level which gives immense flexibility when design a database. Effectively, we are able to provide the whole spectrum of CAP properties, focusing on those which are necessary for a given case.

Chapter 4
NoSQL Benchmarking

In order to assess the performance of non-relational databases, a set of benchmarks has been developed targeting both Riak and Cassandra. A sharded MySQL setup was also benchmarked in order to provide a baseline.

A benchmarking framework was developed to fulfill this purpose. In this section the bench-marking methodology and results are presented. The developed benchmarking framework is also detailed.

Methodology

The methodology presented was based on the work performed by Yahoo! on benchmarking cloud serving systems. The systems were benchmarked according to three different tiers, in order to gain more knowledge on some characteristics relevant to a distributed system.

Tiers

In this section the three benchmark tiers for evaluating the performance, scalability and elasticity of database systems are presented.

Raw Performance

This tier allows us to evaluate the raw performance of read and write operations. The systems were setup in a distributed environment with a randomly generated dataset. On this benchmark the systems were stressed with a progressively increasing load of both read and write operations, i.e. the throughput (operations/second) was increased and the average latency of the requests was monitored. This benchmark was performed under different workload scenarios with different percentages of both read and write operations. These scenarios will be described later. With these benchmarks it will be possible to see how the database scales under increasing load and also under different workload conditions.

Scalability

An important characteristic of a distributed systems is their ability to scale horizontally, i.e. by adding more nodes to the system. Ideally, as we add more nodes to the system it should scale linearly, for example if we double the number of nodes ideally the system should then be able to handle twice the maximum throughput that it was able to handle before. Unfortunately, we know from Amdahl's Law that that is not the case. Distributed systems are limited by the amount of parallel computation that is possible and the mechanisms involved in distributing the system introduce some overhead that degrades performance.

On this benchmark we progressively increase the load on the system and the size of the dataset as the number of nodes is also increased. Allowing us to ascertain how well the system scales as it grows. It's important to note that after adding each node the system was given enough time to stabilize before restarting the benchmark. Therefore, the performance degradation associated with transferring data between nodes in order for it to rebalance is not taken into account.

Elasticity

As stated before, as nodes are added to the system, the system has to rebalance, effectively re-distributing data across the new nodes until it stabilizes. The ability for a distributed system to do so is known as Elasticity, since it is able to seamlessly grow (or shrink) while online, and it is expected to improve performance after the system stabilizes. This process is expected to cause some load on the system and therefore, as the system is rebalancing it's ability to support a certain throughput should decrease, yielding higher latencies to the requests.

On this benchmark, a slightly overloaded and stabilized system is given a constant throughput of requests. After ten minutes a new node is added to the system while the requests are still being made (with the same throughput). A spike in latencies is expected while the system readjusts itself.

This benchmark attempts to mimic the real-world scenario were an overloaded system needs to grow in order to accommodate the increased performance needs. The measures taken will allow us to determine how long the system takes to stabilize after a new node is added and if afterwards it yields better performance.

4.2 Scenarios

In order to test the system under different scenarios two different workloads were used. They vary on the percentage of read and write operations. On Table 4.1 it's possible to see the different read and write probabilities for the two scenarios. Also given on the table is the distribution used to select which objects were to be read or written.

Table 4.1: Tested workload scenarios

	Read Probability	Write Probability	Distribution
Read Heavy	0.95	0.05	Uniform
Write Heavy	0.70	0.30	Uniform

These scenarios attempt to model two different real-world scenarios and they were chosen with regards to the needs of "PT Inovação". The read heavy workload attempts to model the back office operations involved in customer-support. Most of the operations will be to fetch user's data as the operator needs to find the necessary information.

The write heavy scenario attempts to model the operations involved in running telecommuni-cations services. Most of the operations will be to read and fetch user data (e.g. getting the user mobile plan, checking it's balance, etc.) but it will also be necessary to store session and logging information.

The distribution used for selecting objects was a uniform distribution as it is the most ade-quate to the scenarios that the benchmark attempts to model. There are cases where a different distribution would be more appropriate, e.g. zipifian distribution where some records would be more "popular". Still, for example, when dealing with customer-support the probability of any user having a problem and calling customer-support is uniform. With few exceptions, no user is bound to have "more problems" and therefore to be more "popular".

It's important to notice that for the scalability and elasticity benchmarks, only the read heavy scenario was used.

Quantum Bench

In order to be able to perform the benchmarks described before with regards to the different tiers, a benchmarking framework was developed. The purpose of this framework is to provide flexibil-ity regarding the benchmarking process, allowing us to define different workloads with different operations and to be used on different databases. It is of great value to test new systems and to mimic real-world usage, allowing anyone to experiment and predict how a system might behave under a production environment.

The system is responsible for executing the defined operations against the database, generating the specified load and also keeping track of latency measurements.

This framework was written in JRuby, mainly with regards to "PT Inovação"'s technology choices, in order to better reflect a real-world scenario, as this is the technology that would be used in a production environment.

Architecture

The system is composed of three main building blocks: Core, Benchmark and DB Client; as seen in Figure 4.1.

The Core is responsible for executing a defined Benchmark against a database using the pro-vided DB Client. To do so, it maintains a pool of threads that continuously issue requests to the database. The threads are subject to an auto -throttling mechanism in order to make sure that the desired throughput is achieved. Each thread is also responsible for measuring the latency of its operations. These latencies are then used by the statistics module to book the average, minimum, maximum, standard deviation, 95th percentile and 99th percentile latencies.

The Benchmark module is responsible for implementing all the logic that is to be used when defining a new benchmark. It is responsible for providing a single point of entry that each worker thread will execute. This module is easily extensible, all that is necessary is to implement a new Benchmark class with a run() method. In the run() method the user is expected to implement the operations that are to be executed against the database, usually using some probability logic. A core benchmark class is provided, that executes read and update operations against the database with varying probability percentages. As expected, the selection of objects follows a probability distribution.

The DB Client module is responsible for interacting with the database, so that the operations defined in the Benchmark module can be successfully executed. Under this module, three classes were implemented to connect with different databases, namely: Cassandra, Riak and MySQL. If we were to implement a new database client we would have to create a new class and define three methods insert(), read() and update(), responsible for CRU(D) operations against the database.

The Core module takes all the information regarding which benchmark class to use, and what client to use, from a JSON file. Additionally it is also possible possible to define the desired throughput, number of operations or duration (in minutes) of the benchmark. It is also possible to define any arguments necessary to both the benchmark class and the client class that is to be used. For example, the core benchmark class takes the read and write probability as argument when creating the object.

After the benchmark finishes, the Core module creates a log file with all the statistical infor-mation relevant to the benchmark which is saved in a logs folder.

Results

In this section the results of benchmarking the databases are presented. Results are presented for three different databases: Cassandra, Riak and MySQL. Additionally, the experimental setup is detailed as well as the dataset used.

Setup

As a distributed system, the databases had to be setup in a cluster that contained several nodes. This cluster was comprised of virtual machines each hosting one node of the database ring. Each virtual machine, and therefore each node, was given a dual-core processor and 4GB of RAM. Additionally the client node, responsible for running the benchmarking framework and generating the necessary load on the database, was given two quad-core processors and a total of 16GB of RAM. The virtual machines were hosted on a four-blade server where each blade hosted as much as four virtual machines. Each blade sported 2 Xeon X3440 CPUs, 24GB of RAM and a Gigabit network connection. One of the blades was used exclusively to host the benchmark client. The host system was running Debian Linux 8.0 and virtualization was provided by KVM.

Each virtual machine (node) was also running Debian Linux 8.0 and the following versions of the databases were used in the benchmarks:

Riak – 0.14.1

Cassandra – 0.7.5

MySQL – 5.1.49

It's also important to note that replication mechanisms were always disabled (i.e. the repli-cation factor was set to 1). Replication was disabled so that the performance baseline could be measured. Still, it is possible to predict how replication affects performance. Read operation's performance is expected to increase as the replication factor increases, while the write operation's performance is expected to decrease as the system has an additional overhead by having to per-form the same write operation in different nodes. Additionally, the sharded MySQL environment does not provide any replication mechanism. Still, it is out of scope of this work to benchmark and examine the impact of replication on NoSQL databases.

As stated before, the MySQL database was used in a sharded environment. The sharding was performed by using client-side hashing. In this regard, MySQL has a slight advantage over the other databases, since the client always knows on which node a certain object is and therefore it always asks that node directly, whereas on the other databases, distribution is completely trans-parent to the client and therefore, since the client simply asks a node for a given object, that node might not have the object and it may have to route the request to the correct node. As expected, this routing mechanism produces some overhead and is also dependent on network latency.

MySQL was used only for the raw performance benchmarks. As the sharding environment does not provide any mechanisms for transparent distribution of data, it is impossible to measure it's scalability and elasticity.

The raw performances benchmarks were all performed on a 6 node cluster. The scalability benchmarks were done starting with a 6 node cluster and gradually adding nodes until a 12 node cluster was achieved. The elasticity benchmarks were done on a 6 node cluster to which a 7th node was added.

From the experiments performed it was clear that virtual machines are not an ideal deployment platform, especially since IO performance is subpar and it quickly becomes a bottleneck. Therefore the presented results must be interpreted with this caveat in mind.

The dataset comprised of random data generated and allocated into 10 "fields" each of 100 bytes. Therefore, each object was 1 KB in size. Each node housed 1GB of data, i.e. 1 million objects. As the number of nodes increased, so did the dataset. As the performance benchmarks were done on a 6 node cluster the dataset had, subsequently, 6 million records (6 GB). Some initial experiments were performed using 10GB of data per node. Still, it soon showed itself to be impractical due to the poor IO performance of the virtual machines. IO would be a bottleneck that would limit the system to very low throughputs. Therefore the option was taken to reduce the dataset so that the file system would have to ability to cache some of the data and effectively removing (or at least attenuating) the IO bottleneck.

Raw Performance

Performance results are presented in this section according to the two tested workloads: update heavy and read heavy.

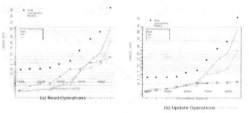

Figure 4.2: Update heavy workload results

Update Heavy Workload

On this benchmark the performance of the databases under an update heavy environment was measured, in this case 30 percent of the operations are updates and the remaining 70 percent are read operations. In figure 4.2 it is possible to observe the average latency of both read and update operations as the load on the system is increased.

As is shown on the figure, for all systems, operation latency increased as the offered throughput increased. Cassandra, which is optimized for write-heavy workloads, provided the lowest latency at high throughputs for both read and update operations. Both Riak and MySQL scaled exponen-tially, achieving similar latency versus throughput curves, especially at lower throughputs. On the other hand, Cassandra scaled linearly, although for the read operations it started with higher laten-cies than the other systems. On both Riak and MySQL update operations always yielded higher latencies than read operations at the same throughput. However, on Cassandra the opposite was observed: update operations were always faster.

Regarding read operations there is not much variance in the results regarding the three systems. However, on update operations there is a high variance across the three systems, especially at higher throughputs (7000 ops/s). At 10000 ops/s Cassandra achieved an average latency of 9.85ms for update operations, 80% less than Riak (48.54ms) and 71% less than MySQL (33.01ms).

It is expected that by increasing the percentage of update operations Cassandra's performance would continue to improve, since it performs write operations more efficiently than read oper-ations, while that of the other systems would deteriorate effectively increasing the performance difference between Cassandra and both MySQL and Riak.

Read Heavy Workload

The read heavy workload puts the databases to stress under a different environment where 95 percent of the operations are reads and the remaining 5 percent are update operations. Figure 4.3 shows latency versus throughput curves for both read and update operations.

Again, it is possible to observe that for all systems, as the throughput increased the average latency also increased as expected.

The scaling curves for update operations were very similar to those achieved on the last bench-mark, although the average latencies were smaller throughout the whole range of offered through-put. MySQL and Riak continued to exhibit exponential growth while Cassandra remained scaling linearly with optimal results for write operations.

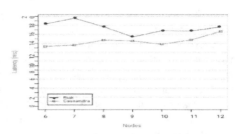

Figure 4.4: Scalability benchmark results

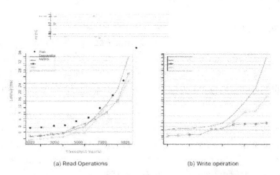

(a) Read Operations   (b) Write operation

Regarding read operations the results are very similar across all systems, all achieving expo-nential growth with resembling curves. Cassandra's performance worsened due to the increase of read operations. Read operations put an extra disk I/O constraint on Cassandra necessary to fetch and assemble records which saturates disk access. At 10000 ops/s MySQL achieved the lowest latency at 27.20ms, just 3ms less than the latencies achieved by Cassandra. As with update opera-tions, when compared to the last benchmark the average latency decreased for all databases except for Cassandra, where the increased read operations led to a performance penalty.

Scalability

For this experiment, the test systems were started with 6 nodes and were continuously increased to a final number of 12 nodes. As the number of nodes was increased the size of dataset and the request rate was also increased proportionally. The read heavy workload was used, and the average latency of read operations was measured.

In figure 4.4 it is possible to see the average read latency for each database as the number of nodes increases. As is possible to ascertain, the average latency is nearly constant indicating that both databases have good scalability properties. Although there are some variations on latency these are very small, the biggest difference being of approximately 4ms, which can be easily attributed to several causes such as network latency, cache misses, etc.

This benchmark demonstrates that both databases are properly prepared to scale out, by adding more nodes to the system as necessary in an effort to ensure the desired performance. In this case it was possible to achieve high throughputs with a desirable low latency. With the highest number of nodes it was possible to stress the systems with as much as 10000 ops/s while maintaining very low latencies, which as was seen on previous benchmarks was not possible with a smaller number of nodes.

Elasticity

On this benchmark the systems were started with 6 nodes and were slightly overloaded both in the dataset size and request rate. Specifically, deriving from the previous scalability benchmark, we used the dataset size and throughput that was used with a 7 node ring. This models a situation where the system is no longer capable of dealing with the offered load and a new node is added in order to scale out and effectively handle the load while keeping the system online. The system was put under constant load for one hour. After the 10 minute mark was hit a 7th node was added to the system and subsequently the databases started readjusting and evenly balancing the load.

In figure 4.5 it is possible to see the average latency of read operations throughout every minute of the benchmark. As soon as the 7th node was added there was a sharp increase in for both databases, which is a direct result of moving data to the new node. There is a direct competition of resources (i.e. disk and network capacity) between serving the incoming requests and performing the rebalancing process.

On Riak latencies were highly variable and erratic throughout the whole rebalancing process. The system took approximately 15 minutes to perform the rebalancing and stabilize. The average request latency throughout this period was approximately 666ms, still, there were some latency peaks, namely, at the 22 minute mark where the average latency was 1939ms. After this process finished and the system was stabilized, performance was comparable to that of a ring that started with 7 nodes.

It is possible to conclude that Riak provides good elasticity, since it was able to scale out in a relatively short time, while keeping the system online and under load and achieving similar the expected performance after the system stabilized. Still, it is important to take into consideration that this process is very intensive and it is expected that the process would take a longer time as the data set grows. On a production environment it is therefore advisable that this process is only performed during periods of expected low load on the system.

Cassandra, seems to provide a more predictable latency variance. After the 7th node is added latency peaks at approximately 1029ms and it continuously decreases until the system stabilizes after 8 minutes. The average latency throughout the process is similar to that of Riak's, yielding an average latency of roughly 622ms.

However, it is very important to take into account that unlike Riak, Cassandra does not au-tomatically balance the nodes evenly. Therefore, after the new node was added it was slightly underutilized compared to the previous nodes since it had less data. In order to completely bal-ance the system the balancing process would have to be run individually for each existing node, in this case, an additional six times. It is expected that to achieve a perfectly balanced ring state (like on Riak), the whole process would take more time on Cassandra.

After the system stabilized, performance was slightly lower than what was expected when comparing to a system that started with 7 nodes. This is a result of the slight underutilization of the new node, which translates on its resources not being totally exploited and straining the remaining nodes with additional load.

Conclusions

The performed benchmarks show that both Cassandra and Riak provide performance on par with a relational database. Cassandra provides much better performance than the remaining systems regarding write operations, and its overall performance is slightly hampered by read operations. Riak's performance was very similar to that of the sharded MySQL implementation.

Both systems were able to efficiently scale horizontally as more nodes were added, maintaining roughly the same performance as the load on the database was continuously increased. They also proved to be very elastic, by allowing the system to easily and rapidly grow, while redistributing data across the nodes. Although Riak took longer to stabilize when a new node was added, the ring was completely balanced afterwards, whereas that was not the case for Cassandra.

Strictly from a performance and capabilities point of view, both Cassandra and Riak proved to be good alternatives to relational databases, as they delivered similar (and in some cases better) performance compared to the baseline while at the same time providing distribution mechanisms that were not present in relational databases.

Chapter 5
Data Modeling

This chapter presents a methodology to modeling data with NoSQL databases. Common design patterns are also documented which present reusable solutions to modeling both relationship and common mechanisms.

Methodology

The relational model is a database model based on first-order predicate logic, which was formu-lated 40 years ago by Edgar F. Codd. It relies on relational algebra, or a higher abstrac-tion language such as SQL, to operate on data. There are known best practices regarding the design of relational databases, such as normalization by using normalization forms (e.g. 3NF or BCNF). The widespread use and popularity of relational databases led to an immense and profound knowledge on how to model data.

NoSQL databases, on the other hand, are relatively new and its inception seems to have started more out of necessity (in the enterprise world) rather than out of research and knowledge from the academic world. Therefore, coming from the relational world, it may not be easy to adapt to the non-relational class of databases, which is very vast and diverse and is a little lacking in literature.

The methodology used when performing data modeling for a NoSQL database is quite contrary to that used on a typical relational database. In a relational database we start with a domain model and develop a physical data model around it (i.e. a schema), usually by normalizing it. By contrast, NoSQL databases usually don't have a schema. Instead, we have a "data-driven" application and therefore we focus on the query model and build our data model around it, in order to efficiently satisfy its needs. Basically, the database will be defined in order to support the demands of the application (by the mean of its queries).

Therefore, before we delve into common design patterns and practices, it is important to thor-oughly analyze the application and it's requirements. It is essential to define the typical use cases in order to detect typical access patterns. By examining interdependencies between different el-ements of data it might allow us to make different design decisions.

For example, by defining cardinalities of relationships and, in the case of one to many or many to many relationships, it is important to estimate how big is the many and how will it grow. Different design decisions might have different effects on performance and may also depend on how the data grows. Essentially, it is important to know the data that is being modeled since, unlike relational databases, there is usually more than one "correct" way to model it. "Knowing your data" will help you make sure that the correct design decisions are made.

Playing the role of the devil's advocate one might say that this approach will cause trouble for the practitioner down the line when new queries come up. In fact, this is an invariable problem in software engineering, requirements are bound to change over time, and in this case the database might not be prepared to answer new queries that are imposed. Given this situation, one might need to reexamine the application's needs and redesign the data model. Still, this is no different from needing additional tables or columns on an RBDMS. The bottom line is: the schema isn't any more static than the queries.

Another key point where non-relational and relational databases differ is regarding normal-ization. As stated before the common practice is to normalize a relational database, in order to eliminate redundancy and therefore avoiding inconsistencies. Conversely, as NoSQL databases do not provide a flexible way to operate on data (i.e. a language like SQL), it is usually necessary to denormalize data in order to be able to comply with all the application's requirements.

To summarize, the common methodology is to start with the expected queries and work the data model from then on while also relying on common design patterns.

Design Patterns

In this section the created design patterns are detailed. These design patterns focus mainly on representing relationships between different elements but also on providing the system with capa-bilities to answer certain queries.

These patterns are divided into three distinct categories: Generic, Riak and Cassandra, which as implied makes them either broadly applicable or specific to a certain database.

Generic

This section presents patterns that may be of use on any database since they rely on concepts that are usually common and provided by any database.

Semantic Key

On any key-value store objects are strictly identified by a key. Given that objects are only identified by a key, in a NoSQL database such as Riak or Cassandra, accessing an object can only be done through its key which the application will have to know ahead of time. These systems do not provide a flexible query language, like SQL, and therefore an integral part of developing the data model is to reflect on how to identify objects.

If we use a generic and arbitrary key, such as an UUID or an autoincrementing integer, it is impossible for the application to know ahead of time the key of a certain object, and therefore it is impossible to fetch it without using auxiliary mechanisms (e.g. an inverted index).

Another alternative is to provide objects with a key that has semantic value, i.e. a key that is related to the object and has a meaning. In that case, it is possible for the application to know the key for a certain object.

For example, let us imagine a case where we are trying to model a User object for a web application. As users usually have to pick a username, in this case the username could be used as the key to a User object. Whenever the application wanted to access a user's information it would just have to provide its username instead of an arbitrary id.

The tradeoff is obvious, keys are not prone to change (at least not without great effort) and therefore business's rules have to make sure that the chosen key cannot change and that it is unique. In the given example it is reasonable to expect that usernames are unique and immutable.

Key Correspondence It is also possible that the key itself does not have a semantic value but that there is a semantic value in the way keys are assigned to different objects. For example, using this notion, it is possible to relate two different objects by assigning them the same key. This approach only works to model one-to-one relationships between objects organized into different units (e.g. buckets or tables) since keys must be unique, but it provides a simple, yet effective, way of relating different concerns while keeping them conceptually separate.

Aggregate Key The key may also be an aggregation of different concepts, i.e. an aggregation of different keys. We could merge two different attributes in order to represent a relationship between these two attributes. Taking as an example the concept of Users, if we were to describe a rela-tionship between two users, the key to identify that relationship could be the fusion of two scalar values, their keys, with a separator, thus creating an aggregate key (e.g. the string "key1:key2").

An aggregate key can also be used to extend key correspondence in order to support one-to-many relationships. We can do so by adding a simple prefix to the key (e.g. an autoincrementing integer), eliminating repeated keys. The tradeoff in this case is that it is simpler to find the one side of the relationship, since it is unique, than it is to find the many side. Still, depending on the use case that might be desirable.

Inverted Index

As presented earlier it is imperative that accesses to a certain object are made through its key. Using a semantic key allows us to deal with this constraint, still it is not without trade-offs which sometimes cannot be supported.

An alternative mechanism to deal with this insufficiency is to create an inverted index on one (or more) of the object's attributes. Usually, these indices will have to be maintained by the application since the database does not provide any mechanism to do so (Cassandra provides a mechanism to index fields which will be discussed later on).

Again, taking on the example of the User object, if we were to use an UUID as a key, using an additional structure (e.g. a table, bucket or column family) we could map the user's attribute that we want to index to its UUID. "Indexing" means that the user's attribute is used as a key to the UUID value, so that we can fetch the UUID value just by having the required user's attribute.

If we were to index the username, using this index it would be possible to answer the following equality predicate:

"What's the UUID of the User whose username is andre?"

Given the UUID it would then be possible to fetch the desired object.

Again, there is also a tradeoff: fetching an object requires two read operations, one to find its key and another one to actually read it.

Similarly, creating a new object also requires two write operations, one to store the object and another to create the index. Still, the benefit is that whatever attribute we choose to index (and identify) an object, it can easily be changed just by updating the index. In the given example, it would give users the opportunity to change their username.

Again, it's important to note that usually, these indices have to be maintained by the application itself which increases complexity.

Composition

Unlike relational schema design, where normalization is the preferred way to deal with relations, the same principle isn't necessarily applicable to NoSQL schema design on all cases. Both for performance and ease of modeling, it may make sense to relate two different concepts by coupling them together. Semantically, this describes a relationship of the type has a, and one of the related objects is represented (and persisted) inside the other object.

As an example, a person might have different addresses. Although these are two different, yet related, entities, they can be coupled and represented as a whole. In Listing 5.1 it's possible to see the aforementioned example where the person is represented as a JSON document. The addresses related to that person are embedded into it's document inside a JSON array.

Still, it's important to note the drawback. It makes sense to couple two different concepts when they are frequently accessed together. Taking on the example, it wouldn't make sense to composite a person and its addresses if we were to continuously access the addresses alone. Good candidates for composition are domain concepts that are very dependent on their "owner" concept and are limited in number.

It's also important to take into account the increased size of the object, as it may affect the database performance.

Lazy Deletion

As seen before, even when dealing with non-relational data, applications, usually, still require relationships to be formed between data in order to interconnect different elements. Invariably,

```
1 {
"name": "Ms. Lavina Cassin",
"gender": "female",
"birth_date": "Sep 05 1953",
"creation_date": "Mon Jun 13 10:38:28 +0100 2011",
"status": "active",
"addresses": [
{
"address": "3458 Keeling Light",
"city": "Lake Joan",
"state": "New York"
},
{
"address": "8624 Elyssa Divide",
"city": "Lake Dahliaview",
"state": "Kentucky"
},
{
"address": "04921 Botsford Avenue",
"city": "Flatleyland",
"state": "Oklahoma"
}
]
}
```

Listing 5.1: Example JSON document using the composition pattern

some relationships are bound to cease to exist, e.g. when one of the related elements is deleted.

On a database that provides referential integrity, as is compulsory on RDBMS, it's easy to deal with this scenario by using a cascade delete, which issues the deletion of an element and all the relationships (i.e. rows) that point to it.

Typically, NoSQL databases do not provide referential integrity and this concern is left to the application developer to implement, if necessary. One way to deal with this problem would be to implement a mechanism similar to a cascade delete. Still, such a mechanism is difficult to implement efficiently on a NoSQL database mainly because relationships are maintained by the application and the database is not aware of them, which means that, unless the application has implemented such a mechanism, there is no way to efficiently know which entities are related. Therefore, implementing a cascade delete could force the application to perform full table scans in order to find out which relationships should be deleted. Such an operation would put a lot of stress on the database (which would tend to increase as the dataset grows).

Another way to deal with this issue is to implement a mechanism named Lazy Deletion, which follows the same principle as the evaluation strategy commonly used in functional programming:

Lazy Evaluation: After a certain element is deleted from the database and a relationship can no longer exist, the deletion of all the associated relationships is delayed until the application (usually at the layer that interacts with the database) tries to make use of that "nonexistent" rela-tionship. Whenever the application tries to "follow" a relationship that no longer exists, since one of the related elements is no longer available, the application is able to notice that the relationship is no longer valid and therefore deletes it.

This way the stress associated with deleting all the related elements is distributed across all the associated accesses instead of being centralized on the moment that the element is deleted.

Of course this mechanism has some drawbacks. At any moment the database might be in an inconsistent state, where some relationships might still be represented where in reality they no longer exist. Fortunately, the application knows how to deal with this inconsistency and the presented deletion semantics might be good enough for most applications. Still, for applications that require the database to always be in a consistent state (i.e. strict consistency) this mechanism is of little help.

Another issue related with this mechanism is that since inexistent relationships are still per-sisted to the database, at any moment the database might hold more records than what is necessary, this results in an inefficient use of disk space which in this case is a tradeoff for performance.

In order to prevent the deprecated data from accumulating, a "garbage collection"-like mech-anism could be implemented in order to, asynchronously, remove unnecessary data. This way the load of this operation would still be effectively distributed to certain periods of time (i.e. when the garbage collection mechanism would run) and this mechanism could coexist with lazy deletion.

Riak

Riak provides a feature which allows us to model relationships with ease. Links can be very powerful and they have an intrinsic value. Still, as they are specific to Riak the following pattern is particularly tied to it.

Links

By using links it is possible to create uni-directional relationships between different objects ex-isting in the system. Using this concept it is possible to represent data as a graph-like structure, which can be easily traversed.

As was stated before links are one-way relationships between two objects (existing in any bucket) that can be annotated with any kind of metadata in the form of a tag attribute. As an example, using this mechanism we would be able to relate two different user objects as being friends, by using a link between them with a friend tag. By using link-walking it is possible to traverse all the links of a certain object to get the objects it relates to. It is also possible to limit this traversal, e.g. by limiting it to links with a certain tag (in the previous example, a friend tag). Link-walking steps can be combined to achieve a more in -depth traversal, e.g. getting the friends of friends.

Listing 5.2 shows how easy it is to implement the previous example link-walk operation using Ruby. Given a user object it is only necessary to call the walk() method, to which a tag (and also other options) can be passed. It also shows how link-walk operations can be chained.

```
1 user_object.walk(:tag => "friend")

2 user_object.walk(:tag => "friend").walk(:tag => "friend)
```

Listing 5.2: Ruby link-walking Example

Links have no semantic value to the database and therefore that logic must be implemented by the application. Links also have no notion of cardinality, for example, if it is intended that a relationship is bi-lateral the application will have to create (and effectively maintain) two links between the related objects, i.e. one which way.

There's also no notion of referential integrity regarding links, they can be easily compared to the way hyperlinks work in HTML. When a resource that an HTML link points to ceases to exist, the hyperlink is not automatically deleted but instead points to a location that no longer makes sense: the link is considered broken. It is the responsibility of the application to fix the broken link.

Links also incur some technical limitations that should be taken into account. Since links are persisted as metadata directly on the object, as the number of links of a given object grows, the size of the object itself also increases, which invariably will have performance implications.

Objects with a large number of links will be slower to load, store and to perform MapReduce operations on.

There's also a limitation when using the RESTful HTTP interface, which currently uses an 8K buffer for incoming requests and limits the number of header fields. Since, on the HTTP API links are represented on the HTTP Link header, this effectively limits the number of links an object may have. This limitation is expected to be resolved in forthcoming versions of Riak, but in the meantime it can be overcome by using one of the other (more efficient) interfaces.

Cassandra

The patterns presented in the following section rely on some the elements of Cassandra's data model. As Cassandra's data model is based on BigTable some of the patterns presented can be reused in databases that also follow a similar data model such as HBase, Hypertable or BigTable itself.

Materialized Views

An integral part of relational databases is the ability to JOIN different concepts and also to filter results by a certain attribute, for example by using a WHERE clause. NoSQL databases usually do not provide a way to query data with this degree of flexibility. Therefore, it is necessary to structure the data model for it to be able to answer the desired queries.

A Materialized View contains the results of a certain query and this mechanism is often pro-vided by RDBMS. It is possible to mimic this behavior on Cassandra, at the application-level, by storing and maintaining (denormalized) data in a different column family. For example, given a User object which has a nationality attribute, we may want to query users on their nation-ality. We can do so by creating (and maintaining) a UserByNationality column family that stores user data, having as key the nationality and several columns for each user with that nationality. We can then query this column family for finding all the users with a certain nationality. The same principle can be used to relate two different concepts, in essence, a join table.

Regarding WHERE-like clauses, Cassandra provides the ability to mimic this behavior by creating secondary indexes (with some tradeoffs) which will be discussed later.

Valueless Column

Extending on the previous example of Materialized Views, since we're using the view to store reference data, columns on that column family do not need values. We can use the column name to store the data we want, e.g. a reference object id, and keep the column value empty. In essence, columns don't have any meaningful value, we are just using them as a list. In this case, a row with a key "Portuguese" would have a set of columns each having as it's name the key of a User object.

Valueless Subcolumn: It is also possible to use a SuperColumn in a similar fashion, to store a view, inside the object itself. Subcolumns would be used equally as a list of reference data.

Still, it is important to be cautious when using SuperColumns. Internally, Cassandra has two levels of indexing, key and column. But in SuperColumns there is a third level, subcolumns, which is not indexed. Therefore, any request for a subcolumn deserializes all the subcolumns in that SuperColumn. It is advisable to avoid situations that require a large number of subcolumns.

Secondary Indexes

Starting with version 0.7 of Cassandra, the ability to index column values was introduced. The introduction of secondary indexes allows the application to efficiently query specific values using equality predicates.

Assuming an object that models users which has a nationality attribute, indexing this attribute enables the database to answer a query like:

"Show me all the users from Portugal."

This new feature allows the application to perform complex queries to the database instead of simple accesses by key, without the application having to implement any of the mechanisms (or patterns) detailed earlier. It effectively removes complexity from the application layer since it no longer has to deal with creating and maintaining indexed data.

Secondary indexes should not be relied on for all scenarios though. Since they are imple-mented as a local index they work better for low cardinality fields. For example, a binary field like gender would be an appropriate attribute to index using this scheme. In contrast, a username attribute would not be a good fit for a secondary index since a lot of unique values are expected.

Dealing with Inconsistency

Keeping in mind the CAP Theorem, NoSQL databases tend to trade Consistency for Availability, when compared to traditional relational databases, providing only Eventual Consistency. It is therefore of extreme importance to acknowledge inconsistency and learn how to deal with it.

Some NoSQL databases, such as Cassandra and Riak, allow us to vary the degree of consis-tency required on the operation level, effectively providing both eventual consistency or strong consistency when desired (with an obvious performance penalty).

In order to deal with inconsistency, the first step is to study data access patterns and usage to identify which elements of the data model are bound to need strong consistency and which can get by with eventual consistency without affecting the business logic. Data elements and operations which need strong consistency could then rely on mechanisms given by the database to enforce them (i.e. defining strict consistency levels for certain operations).

Taking as an example the well-known social networking service Twitter, whenever a user creates a new tweet. eventual consistency in the form of read your writes consistency doesn't disrupt the business logic, i.e. whenever a user creates a new tweet it isn't strictly necessary for every other user to also see this change immediately. On the other hand, any form of billing service usually requires strict consistency.

It is also important to mention that usually these systems do not provide a transaction system and therefore not guaranteeing that a set of operations is serializable. This could be achieved by us-ing an additional system to provide distributed coordination, such as Apache ZooKeeper. Still, this behavior would have to be supported on the application layer as no official support exists from the database. There are some projects working on this area, like Cages, which uses ZooKeeper to provide distributed locking and synchronization.

Chapter 6
Case Study

This chapter presents a case study that serves as a proof of concept for the technology and methods discussed earlier. Two prototypes were implemented using two different databases namely, Cassandra and Riak.

The chapter starts by describing the domain problem that the prototypes try to address. The implementation for both databases is then presented, describing the patterns and mechanisms used.

Finally, an analysis on both implementations is presented. A benchmark is presented, with an alternative relational implementation using MySQL, to serve as a baseline.

Problem Description

As this text was developed for "PT Inovação"'s, the selected case study is in the context of the company's business.

The case study focuses on a simplified model of a telecommunications operator, mainly di-rected at supporting backoffice operations, such as customer support, but also assisting some of the processes related to the telecommunications services provided (e.g. mobile telephony).

As seen in Figure 6.1, the system is comprised of six main entities:

Customer – The customer is the real-life recipient of the services provided. It can be either an individual or a corporate customer (i.e. a company). The customer must be identifiable in the real-world and to that extent it has associated with it legal documents and contact channels (e.g. email, address, telephone number). Customers can relate with each other, either for providing specialized services, or just for facilitating internal business intelligence.

Account – An account is the unit used internally to associate a customer with the services provided and used. It is possible that a customer may have many accounts (e.g. a corporate customer may have many accounts, one for each of its employees).

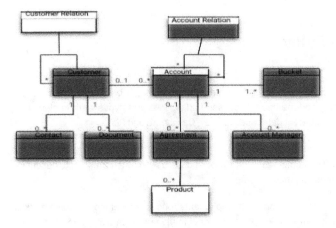

Figure 6.1: Simplified telecommunications operator data model

Account Manager – The account manager, as the name implies, is an internal employee responsible for supporting and managing a certain account.

Product – A product is a service provided by the telecommunications operator, which can be a simple voice service, Internet access, etc. This unit represents the subscription by a certain account of a product, usually identifying when the product was subscribed, how long it is valid for and the status of the subscription.

Agreement – Product subscriptions are mediated through an agreement between an account and the service provider. This entity models that agreement which defines the terms of service. It serves as the connection between an account and the services it is able to use.

Bucket – Associated with an account is a unit that allows it to be billed on the services it uses. A bucket, maintains the balance associated with an account and it's where the service usage is credited.

It's also important to notice that accounts may also relate with each other. These relationships allow them to define a tree structure that enables the sharing of products (i.e. by sharing agree-ments) and buckets. For example, a corporate customer might define top-level accounts for each of its cost centers giving each employee a child account for the given cost center. Buckets and

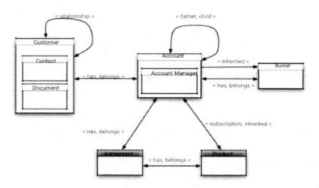

Figure 6.2: Riak's data model

products could be shared across all the accounts of a cost center, which enables a more dynamic control over subscribed services and associated costs.

Although the relationship details can be elaborated on a relationship basis, usually it's a fa-ther/child relationship where the child inherits all the buckets and products associated with its father account. To keep matters simple, this father/child is assumed to be the only type of relation-ship between accounts. It is also important to note that this inheritance is transitive, i.e. the child account also inherits the buckets and products subscribed by its "grandfather" account.

Implementation

In this section the two developed prototypes for Riak and Cassandra are presented. These two prototypes were developed by relying on the methodology and design patterns presented earlier. Implementation details and design decisions are presented and discussed, justifying the use of the chosen design patterns.

Riak

The Riak implementation relied mainly on two patterns: links and composition. All the objects are serialized using JSON, which allows for a flexible schema-free representation.

In Figure 6.2 it is possible to see a representation of the data model modified for Riak. Each entity maps to a Riak object stored in a different bucket with the exception of objects that are enclosed inside another object. To such objects, the composition pattern was applied and therefore they are stored inside the enclosing object. The various arrows represent links between objects.

As stated before customers can be of differing types, each having different attributes, still since we're using a schema-free representation it is possible to use the same entity to represent the various types. As seen in Listing 6.1 there is a type attribute to identify which type of customer is represented.

```
1  {
2    "id": 6,
3    "type": "individual",
4    "name": "Garett Lynch",
5    "gender": "male",
6    "birth_date": "Mon Aug 27 1992",
7    "nationality": "Portuguese",
8    "segment": "youth",
9    "creation_date": "Mon Jun 13 11:20:31 +0100 2011",
10   "status": "active",
11   "contacts": [
12     {
13       "type": "fax",
14       "number": "(885)576-4626 x839"
15     },
16     {
17       "type": "telephone",
18       "number": "1-415-413-1986"
19     }
20   ],
21   "documents": [
22     {
23       "type": "driving_license",
```

```
24      "number": "120622047",
25      "category": "A"
26   }
27  ]
28 }
```

Listing 6.1: Example customer document

Both contacts and addresses were composited and stored inside the customer object itself using JSON arrays. These entities are very tightly coupled to the customer object and are prone to be accessed as a whole, therefore it makes sense to store them together. The same principle was applied to the account manager, which is stored inside the account object.

As seen before, all the relationships between the different entities are represented as links, so that we can effortlessly traverse a graph structure as necessary. Clients relate to each other by using a link between Customer objects with a tag identifying relationship types.

There are also links between a Customer and it's associated Accounts, denoting the inherent "has/belongs to" relationship. The same principle is also applied to Agreements, Products and Buckets. It is important to notice that although these links represent two-way relationships, they have to be persisted as two separate links each with its own tags (and each on a different direction).

As explained before, the subscription to a product is mediated through an agreement. Still, has the system will usually check if an account has subscribed to a certain service it makes sense to denormalize this relationship in order to achieve better performance. Therefore, there is also a link directly between the account and the product to denote a subscription.

Since products and buckets can be inherited, whenever an account tries to use a service, if it has a father account, the system will have to check the father account buckets and its associated services, as well as other accounts higher in the chain. This process involves traversing the tree and would not be able to achieve the desired performance. Again the solution, is to denormalize the necessary data. To this extent there is a link between the child account and the buckets and products it inherited from its father account as well as from all the accounts higher in the hierarchy. These links are denoted with a dashed line in Figure 6.2, as they are denormalized information.

All of the objects use an UUID as a key since the application's requirements didn't allow the use of a semantic key.

Although not represented on the diagram, an inverted index for customers was kept, usually indexing a unique legal document that identified the customer (e.g. identity card number). The customer is therefore used as the "point of entry" to the system.

Cassandra

In figure 6.3 it is possible to see a representation of data model used in Cassandra. First of all, since this representation is not standard it is important to clarify it. Every table represents either a ColumnFamily or a SuperColumnFamily. In the table header there is a trailing symbol that allows us to distinguish each case, the symbols being CF for a ColumnFamily and SCF for a SuperColumnFamily.

The key that identifies the object is represented by RowKey . Inside the table the columns are specified by their name. In the case of SuperColumnFamilies, SuperColumns are identified by

SuperColumnName and the subcolumns that are part of it are given below.

On some situations the symbol ". . . " is represented inside a table. Since Cassandra is schema-free regarding columns, the triple-dot means that additional columns, similar to the ones presented, could be added.

Specification aside, we can now analyze the given data model. Customer information is stored in the Customer SuperColumnFamily on a supercolumn named info which has subcolumns for all the relevant and necessary attributes. Again, as Cassandra is schema-free regarding columns, depending on the type of customer these subcolumns may vary. The valueless subcolumn pattern was used to maintain the relationships between the customer and its associated entities, namely: Documents, Contacts and Accounts. There is one supercolumn for each of these entities were the keys of the related objects can be added.

Documents and contacts are maintained each in a simple ColumnFamily.

<<SCF>> Customer

<<RowKey>> #customerUUID

<<SuperColumnName>> info +name

+type

+segment

+status +creation_date

<<SuperColumnName>> contacts +contact1UUID

+contact2UUID +...

<<SuperColumnName>> documents +document1UUID

+document2UUID +...

<<SuperColumnName>> accounts +account1UUID

+account2UUID +...

   <<SCF>> CustomerRelation

<<RowKey>> #customerUUID

<<SuperColumnName>> tag1 +customer1UUID +customer2UUID

+...

<<SuperColumnName>> tag2 +customer3UUID +customer4UUID

+..<<CF>> Document

<<RowKey>> #documentUUID +desc

+issue_date +expire_date +type +customerUUID

   <<CF>> Contact

<<RowKey>> #contactUUID +desc

+schedule

+subject

+type

+customerUUID

   <<CF>> AccountManager

<<RowKey>> #managerUUID +name

+contact_reason +priority +accountUUID

 <<CF>> AgreementsByAccount

<<RowKey>> #accountUUID +agreement1UUID +agreement2UUID

+...

 <<CF>> ProductsByAccount

 <<RowKey>> #accountUUID +product1UUID +product2UUID

 +...

 <<CF>> BucketsByAccount

 <<RowKey>> #accountUUID +bucket1UUID +bucket2UUID

<<SCF>> Account

<<RowKey>> #accountUUID

<<SuperColumnName>> info +external_id

+status

+language

+desc +creation_date +customerUUID

<<SuperColumnName>> managers +account_manager1UUID
+account_manager2UUID

+...

<<SuperColumnName>> buckets +bucket1UUID

+bucket2UUID +...

<<SuperColumnName>> father +account1UUID

<<SuperColumnName>> children +account1UUID

+account2UUID +...

<<SCF>> Agreement

<<RowKey>> #agreementUUID

<<SuperColumnName>> info +spec

+accountUUID

<<SuperColumnName>> products +product1UUID

+product2UUID +...

<<CF>> Product

<<RowKey>> #productUUID +spec

+subscription_date +status

+valid_for +agreementUUID

<<CF>> Bucket

<<RowKey>> #bucketUUID +type

+amount +valid_start_date +valid_end_date +accountUUID

Figure 6.3: Cassandra's data model

Relationships between customers are maintained in the CustomerRelation SuperColumnFam-ily. In this SuperColumnFamily there is one SuperColumn for each relationship type that a cus-tomer might have. Under each type the valueless subcolumn pattern is used to list the keys of the related customers.

Accounts are stored in a SuperColumnFamily with an approach identical to that of customers, that is, there is a SuperColumn info where all the attributes of the Account are stored and the valueless subcolumn is again used to maintain the objects directly related with the account, in this case, the associated account managers, buckets, the father account and children accounts.

It is important to notice that the buckets SuperColumn in the Account SuperColumnFamily only stores the keys of buckets directly assigned to that account and therefore not buckets that were inherited.

To that extent, since it is a common use case to ask for all the buckets related to an account (either directly or inherited) a ColumnFamily BucketsByAccount was created, using the Materialized View and Valueless Column pattern. It uses the account key as its key (semantic key correspondence), and it lists all the buckets ids related with that account. Since the number of all buckets related to an account might be high (and it is expected to increase) due to the software limitations related to SuperColumns it makes sense to keep this information in a separate Colum-nFamily (as opposed to using the Valueless Subcolumn pattern). The same principle was applied to Products and Agreements and thus the ColumnFamilies ProductsByAccount and Agreements-ByAccount were created in order to efficiently retrieve all the products and agreements associated with an account.

Buckets and Products are stored in separate ColumnFamilies each maintaining it's related attributes. Both the Product and Bucket have respectively the agreement key and account key to which they belong, which serves as a foreign key, although no referential integrity is enforced.

Finally, agreements are stored in a SuperColumnFamily which stores all of the agreement in-formation in a SuperColumn info and the related products are stored in the products SuperColumn using the Valueless Subcolumn pattern.

As with Riak, all the keys are UUIDs and an inverted index was kept on the customer.

Analysis

In this section a performance analysis of the implemented prototypes is presented. This analysis was carried out by benchmarking both prototypes against a set of common (and expensive) oper-ations. Additionally, a relational implementation based on MySQL is also presented in order to establish a baseline for comparison.

Benchmarking

In order to compare the performance of the implemented prototypes they were benchmarked against six use cases:

Fetching all the customers related with a customer;

Fetching all the child accounts of an account;

Fetching all the "grandchild" accounts of an account;

Fetching all the "grand-grandchild" accounts of an account;

Fetching all the directly related buckets of an account;

Fetching all the buckets of an account (directly related and inherited).

In addition to both the Cassandra and Riak implementations a relational MySQL implemen-tation was also provided in order to serve as a baseline for comparison. This implementation followed the relational model strictly by making sure that the data model was properly normal-ized.

For all the benchmarks, the size of the dataset was increased exponentially and the average latency of each request was measured for each varying degree of dataset size.

Unlike the previous benchmarks, these tests were performed on a single node. In this case, as MySQL was used as a baseline, useful for comparing to a traditional relational database imple-mentation, it was necessary to make use of all the relational capabilities (e.g. JOIN statements, referential integrity, etc.) which were not available on a sharded environment. To keep the test-ing environment as simple as possible, and also due to the unavailability of the previously used infrastructure this decision was taken.

It is important to note that Riak has a bug that prevents it from performing link-walking oper-ations when the replication factor is set to 1[1], which was the case when running on a single node. Therefore, Riak was setup with two nodes running on the single host that was used for all the other experiments. Computing resources available to each database were the same, however this caveat should be taken into account when evaluating Riak's results, as it was put on an detrimental situation.

Customers

For this benchmark the number of existing customers was continuously increased and the average latency of getting the related customers was measured. Each customer was related with at least two customers but, as the number of customers increased, so did the number of relations.

In Figure 6.4 the results of this benchmark are shown.

To fetch all the related customers, Riak uses link-walking since there is a link between related customers. On Cassandra, the CustomerRelation ColumnFamily is used to get the keys of the related customers and then a multiget is issued to get those objects. On MySQL there is a join table to relate customers and therefore a JOIN statement is issued to get all the related customers.

On Riak we can see that, as the number of customers grows exponentially, so does the time it takes to perform the query. Cassandra issues a similar result, although this growth is only substantial on the last increase of customers. This growth is also visible on MySQL, still it's as pronounced. The JOIN is performed on indexed keys and therefore MySQL yield excellent performance since it does not rely on full table scans.

Child Accounts

For the following benchmarks, the ramification factor of the accounts tree was continuously in-creased. By increasing the ramification factor each account had more child and thus the total number of accounts was increased. The accounts tree was always complete, i.e. if the ramifica-tion factor was set to N all the accounts had exactly N child accounts (except for the last level). The height of this tree was fixed to 3. Each account had 3 direct buckets, still, as the number of

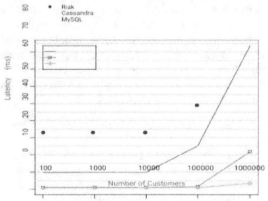

Figure 6.4: Customer benchmarking results

accounts grew the number of inherited buckets also increased.

All the benchmarks test the worst-case scenario, i.e. the case which most likely yields the worst performance, in order to make sure that all benchmarks are even and fair given the associated randomness. For example, when fetching the "grand-grandchild" of an account, given that the three has a depth of 3, the worst case scenario is using the root of the tree. When fetching all the

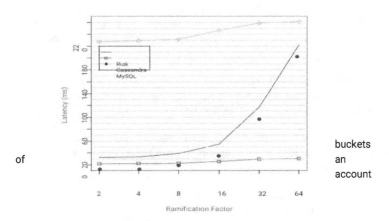

of

buckets
an
account

Figure 6.5: Child accounts benchmarking results

(including inherited) the worst-case scenario is a leaf account, since it has the most buckets.

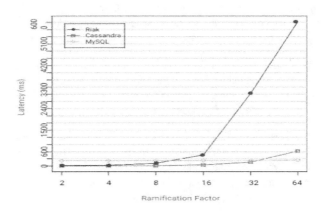

Figure 6.6: "Grandchild" accounts benchmarking results

Figure 6.5 presents the results of fetching child accounts.

The account hierarchy is modeled as an adjacency list and therefore, getting the child accounts on MySQL involves calling a stored procedure that performs a depth-first search, by iteratively executing a JOIN operation between the Account table and the join table used to maintain account relationships. This method allows for getting all the descendents of an account at a certain depth, in this case the depth is 1.

On Riak, again, it's just a simple link-walking operation. On Cassandra the child account keys are fetched from the children SuperColumn on the Account object and then a multiget statement is issued to retrieve all of the children accounts.

Link-walking on Riak scales exponentially as the number of accounts grows. Still, even at the highest ramification factor it is lower than the results achieved with MySQL.

There is an inherent overhead with using the aforementioned stored procedure (~200ms) on MySQL. Still, it is also possible to note a slight increase in latency as the ramification factor increase

On Cassandra this operations seems to scale linearly with a very little increase even as the number of accounts increases exponentially. The performance achieved with the highest ramifica-tion factor is significantly lower than that of the other databases.

"Grandchild" Accounts

This benchmark is similar to the previous the only difference being that the search depth was increased and the operation should therefore yield a higher number of results. The results of this benchmark are presented in Figure 6.6.

On Riak this operation involves a two-step link-walking, while on Cassandra it involves a depth-first search similar to the one performed on MySQL's stored procedure. Still, this logic is implemented on the application and therefore it involves multiple round-trips to the database.

Again, the results achieved with Riak are similar. The scaling was identical, although, as expected the absolute values were much higher. MySQL, despite, the initial overhead when using the stored procedure scaled well, achieving the best performance on the last test case with the highest ramification factor.

Cassandra's performance degrades significantly as compared to the last benchmark. This can be attributed to the additional search logic that runs on the application side. Although it is similar to the one used on MySQL it is implemented in Ruby which is not as performant as the MySQL implementation (based on a C API). Additionally, the multiple round-trips necessary also have a toll on performance.

"Grand-grandchild" Accounts

The issues presented on the last benchmark were exacerbated on this benchmark, since increasing the depth also increases the number of resulting accounts exponentially (given by $ramification\_factor^{depth}$) as is visible in Figure 6.7.

On Riak this operation involved a three-step link-walk. Riak was unable to perform the op-eration past the ramification factor of 16. Presumably, because the Erlang VM, responsible for running Riak, ran out of allocated heap memory.

Similarly, Cassandra was only able to perform the operation upto a ramification factor of 32. Again, the VM responsible for running the application code (in this case the JVM as JRuby was used) ran out of heap memory. Still, it is possible to assert that both Riak and Cassandra results would keep increasing exponentially.

None of the databases was able to provide satisfactory results for the highest ramification factor that they were able to support.

Direct Buckets

This benchmark involves getting all the buckets that are directly related to an account. On MySQL a JOIN statement is issued, joining the bucket and account data on the (indexed) account id. Yet again, on Riak the operation is performed using link-walking, following the links from the account to its buckets. On Cassandra, it relies on getting the bucket's keys that are stored on the buckets

SuperColumn inside the Account object.

As shown in Figure 6.8, Cassandra provides the lowest latency and it performs consistently as the ramification factor increases. It is important to notice that as the ramification factor increases, the number of directly related buckets is still the same. Still, the overall number of buckets and

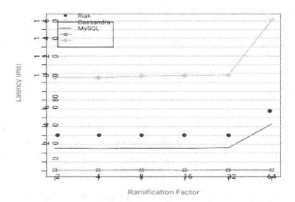

Figure 6.9: Inherited buckets benchmarking results

accounts increases. This doesn't overall increase of the data set doesn't affect Cassandra as keys are accessed directly.

Still, on both Riak and MySQL performance is affected with the highest ramification factor. On Riak, the link-walking operation as to be performed over a larger keyspace. On MySQL, the

JOIN operation has to be performed on tables with more data and even though the joined columns are indexed, there is a slight increase in latency.

Inherited Buckets

To get all the buckets of an account (including inherited) on MySQL a stored procedure performs a "bottom-up" search starting with the selected account and fetching all the buckets of the related accounts higher in the hierarchy. Again, as we can see in Figure 6.9, there is some overhead involved in using stored procedures (~100ms) and latency scales exponentially with the highest ramification factor.

Both on Riak and Cassandra this information is denormalized. In the case of Riak there are links from the Account to Buckets with an inherited tag, therefore, a link-walk operation is able to fetch all the expected buckets. On Cassandra this information lies on the BucketsByAccount

ColumnFamily, and again, all the bucket keys are directly available and all that is necessary is to perform a multiget operation to fetch all the buckets.

Both Riak and Cassandra seem to scale linearly on this benchmark, although Riak yields slightly higher latencies with the highest ramification factor. It's possible to see that link-walking has some associated overhead. Still, it produces consistent results even as the ramification factor increases. Cassandra yields very low latencies which are also stable as the dataset increases.

Conclusions

This case study illustrates the adoption of NoSQL systems to a real-world scenario, it's possible to see the advantages but also the associated drawbacks. Performance wise, both Cassandra and Riak yield good results, on some situations achieving better results than the MySQL solution used as a baseline.

The Riak implementation relied mainly on using links to maintain relationships. Links are a very natural and expressive way to represent relationships and by relying on link-walking it is easy to traverse the whole data model in a simple yet flexible way. Still, has shown by the benchmarks the extreme reliance on link-walking incurs some performance penalties.

Cassandra represented most relationships by means of denormalization. It is therefore able to achieve very good results as there is no need to "compute" the results of a relationship. One might say that the techniques used could also be applied to a relational database, in this case to MySQL, in order to achieve better performance. That is certainly true, one might for example perform de-normalization in the same way employed by Cassandra. Using this concrete example, one could store all of the inherited buckets of an account in a separate table, reducing the need for expensive computation. Still, normalization is the norm in a relational database. NoSQL databases lack on relational features in order to provide other benefits in return (e.g. easy scalability, improved avail-ability). If one keeps "abusing" a relational database (e.g. denormalization, sharding), we might then find that we've lost some of the most important features provided by a relational database (e.g. referential integrity, join operations, etc.), eventually ending up with a NoSQL-like database but without the added benefits.

As both Riak and Cassandra rely on denormalization, there is a trade-off between performance and space. As an example, considering the data set with 1 million customers, that dataset took up 1.6GB on MySQL, 1.7GB on Cassandra (+5%) and 4GB on Riak (+60%). The large space took up by Riak can be justified by an inefficient data serialization format compared to the other databases (i.e. JSON) and also by the large quantities of metadata that must be persisted with each object (to store links). This trade-off must be kept in mind, still, the small increase of space on Cassandra makes it very cost efficient.

Both prototypes can still be improved, by refining the data model and trying different design decisions. The design of the data model has explicit repercussions on performance and the way data is accessed, therefore it is expected that it is continuously adjusted and properly tested.

Losing a flexible querying system, like SQL, is a huge drawback. The developer has increased responsibilities in both designing the data model but also by maintaining additional duties at the application-level (e.g. referential integrity). It is expected that the developed work will facilitate the adoption of both Riak and Cassandra. Still, such a drastic paradigm shift, as is NoSQL, will require additional effort.

In order to facilitate adoption it might be sensible to use a NoSQL database in order to com-plement a relational system, having the NoSQL database focus on a subset of the domain problem.

It is also important to mention that there is still room for improvement in both Riak and Cas-sandra, and both these technologies keep improving at a fast pace, providing new features that make adoption easier and also providing performance improvements.

Chapter 7
Conclusions and Future Work

Conclusions

NoSQL databases are still a relatively new and flourishing technology. There is a wide array of options, which keeps expanding, and these databases keep changing and improving at a fast pace. With the advent of cloud computing and immense scalability needs, NoSQL databases, with their capabilities to seamlessly scale out, are becoming increasingly popular.

This technological boom also brings forth one of major drawback: as the landscape is so broad it is not easy to determine which database to use for a given situation, and also how to use it, as they usually differ from the concepts associated with traditional relational databases. This work aims to provide valuable knowledge in selecting a NoSQL database and using it efficiently.

In this text a brief analysis of a set of NoSQL databases was made as part of exploring the state of the art. Two of these databases were chosen to be further explored and dissected. A set of benchmarks was performed, allowing us to get a clearer view of both Cassandra and Riak with regards to performance, scalability and elasticity. The developed benchmarking framework also allows a developer to easily test other NoSQL databases, performing experiments that might be relevant when deciding which database to use, but also when tuning and configuring a production system.

The experience and knowledge gained with both Cassandra and Riak was solidified in the form of design patterns, that will show themselves useful when designing a data model for each of these databases. This knowledge was put to test by developing a case study, where these two databases were used. In this case study it is possible to see how the aforementioned design patterns and methodology could be used in a real-world scenario. The resulting implementations were properly tested and benchmarked while also comparing to a traditional relational implementation.

All of the established objectives were successfully achieved. As a result, it is expected that given this work it will be easier to adopt NoSQL databases, as it aims to provide an overview of NoSQL databases as well as the associated and underlying theory.

Data modeling might be-come easier for newcomers by having declared a simple yet pragmatic methodology as well as by defining some common design patterns.

Future Work

There are still a lot of research possibilities to further this study. This project focused mainly on two databases: Cassandra and Riak. Still, a large number of NoSQL databases exists, each build-ing on different aspects, that could also be studied, for example, by extending the set of bench-marks to other databases. Further study of other databases would also allow for the identification of new design patterns, specific to each database.

The benchmarks could also be extended in order to include different workload scenarios, by varying the percentage of read and write operations but also by using different distributions for selecting objects other than the uniform distribution. Additionally, as these benchmarks were per-formed on a non-ideal environment (e.g. virtualization), it would be desired to repeat the bench-marks using an infrastructure akin to that used in a production environment (i.e. dedicated physical servers, RAID capabilities, etc.) in order to collect more meaningful results.

Moreover, new benchmarks could also be created in order to test different capabilities of the databases such as, replication and fault-tolerance. Regarding replication it would be useful to measure the impact that replication has on performance. It would also be interesting to ascertain how these databases deal with failure, by introducing different faults on a live system (e.g. taking a node down, partitioning the network), it would be possible to measure any resulting errors and performance impact.

It would also be useful to study and develop object-relational mapping capabilities (or object-document mapping, since we're not dealing with relational databases) in order to use these databases, seamlessly, in an object-oriented environment. Specifically, targeting the popular web framework Ruby on Rails[1] it would be practicable to implement a mechanism similar to ActiveRecord by relying and extending the capabilities provided by ActiveModel. It would also be possible to implement some of the detailed design patterns on the "ORM" itself, allowing developers to easily use them while delegating the implementation to the underlying mapping layer.

References

[10g09]   Inc. 10gen. The MongoDB NoSQL Database Blog - BSON, May 2009.   http://
           blog.mongodb.org/post/114440717/bson, last accessed on January 2011.

[10g11a]   Inc. 10gen. Advanced Queries - MongoDB, 2011. http://www.mongodb.org/
           display/DOCS/Advanced+Queries, last accessed on January 2011.

[10g11b]   Inc. 10gen.   Collections - MongoDB,   2011.   http://www.mongodb.org/
           display/DOCS/Collections, last accessed on January 2011.

[10g11c]   Inc. 10gen.   MapReduce - MongoDB, 2011.   http://www.mongodb.org/
           display/DOCS/MapReduce, last accessed on January 2011.

[10g11d]   Inc. 10gen. MongoDB, 2011. http://www.mongodb.org/, last accessed on Jan-
           uary 2011.

[10g11e]   Inc. 10gen.   Object IDs - MongoDB, 2011.   http://www.mongodb.org/
           display/DOCS/Object+IDs, last accessed on January 2011.

[10g11f]   Inc. 10gen.   Replica Sets - MongoDB, 2011.   http://www.mongodb.org/
           display/DOCS/Replica+Sets, last accessed on January 2011.

[10g11g]   Inc. 10gen.   Replication - MongoDB,   2011.   http://www.mongodb.org/
           display/DOCS/Replication, last accessed on January 2011.

[10g11h]   Inc. 10gen. Schema Design - MongoDB, 2011.   http://www.mongodb.org/
           display/DOCS/Schema+Design, last accessed on January 2011.

[10g11i]   Inc. 10gen.   SQL to Mongo Mapping Chart - MongoDB, 2011.   http:
           //www.mongodb.org/display/DOCS/SQL+to+Mongo+Mapping+Chart,
           last accessed on January 2011.

[ALS10]   J. Chris Anderson, Jan Lehnardt, and Noah Slater. CouchDB: The Definitive Guide.
           O'Reilly Media, Inc., 2010.

[Amd67]   Gene M. Amdahl. Validity of the single processor approach to achieving large scale
           computing capabilities. In Proceedings of the April 18-20, 1967, spring joint computer
           conference, AFIPS '67 (Spring), pages 483~485, New York, NY, USA, 1967. ACM.

[BK10]   Nguyen Ba Khoa.   BigTable   Model with Cassandra and HBase,
           2010.   http://aio4s.com/blog/2010/11/08/technology/
           bigtable-model-cassandra-hbase.html,   last accessed on February
           2011.

www.ingramcontent.com/pod-product-compliance
Lightning Source LLC
LaVergne TN
LVHW051711050326
832903LV00032B/4145